Indian Summers

In Sopchoppy

George Scott Strickland

Strickvan Ventures LLC

Depicted events and characters are drawn from personal 40-year-old memories of experiences as a 10–17-year-old boy and may differ from other accounts.

Library of Congress Control Number: 2026905064

Paperback ISBN: 979-8-9950483-0-5

Ebook ISBN: 979-8-9950483-1-2

Book Cover Photo by George Scott Strickland

Illustrations by George Scott Strickland

1st edition 2026

Contents

Dedication

This book is dedicated to my mom Sandra, stepfather Russell, my dad George Ed and stepmother Leona. Without their love, collaboration and support, my life and this book would not have been possible.

Acknowledgements

I would like to thank my wife Lisa for her love and patience in allowing me to write this book. Her willingness to listen to and read countless stories about the town I grew up in was instrumental to getting this book published.

Map of Sopchoppy

Sopchoppy 1975

The conversation usually goes like this:

"Where are you from?" A new acquaintance might ask.

"Sopchoppy, Florida" I answer, giving the town's name where I grew up.

"SLOPchoppy!!??" they question me.

"No, SOPchoppy, there is no L", I correct them.

"Where is that!!??" is the next inevitable question.

Over the last fifty years, I've had this conversation with hundreds of people. The "new acquaintance" has been a job interviewer, a college professor, a new co-worker, a new neighbor, a new dentist, etcetera. Each time, after correcting their pronunciation, I explained where Sopchoppy is located.

Sopchoppy is a very small town found thirty-five miles south of Florida's capital city, Tallahassee. I spent much of my childhood and young adult years there. To some, Sopchoppy is almost mythical - like Andy Griffith's Mayberry. When I tell people stories about it, they don't believe me. How can a small town like this exist? A town where everyone knows everyone? Where so many colorful characters co-exist. A small town where the biggest holiday is the Fourth of July. A place where their biggest festival is about coaxing earthworms out of the ground. It sounds made up! Heck, even the name sounds made up.

Situated in Wakulla County, near the Apalachicola Forest. Sopchoppy is naturally isolated from other nearby towns. It's on Highway 319, and you'll miss it if you drive too quickly. This is because the main part of town isn't on the highway. The highway curves and banks sharply as you approach the town, suggesting that you should just continue your journey without stopping. As if the town is saying, "nothing to see here". You catch a glimpse of a "Welcome to Sopchoppy" sign, a gas station, and then you're back in the woods.

To get into the downtown area of Sopchoppy you must slow down and not go around the curve. You jump off the road before the gas station at the "Y" and go straight instead. After traveling a block or two, you come to a few old buildings: a large Florida Cracker house with bushes growing to the roof, a train depot with no tracks, a small grocery store with a single door entrance. A tiny building with a glass front across from the grocery store.

"Is this really a town?" You might ask.

When I lived in Sopchoppy in the late '70s and early 80's, the closest traffic light was forty miles away in Tallahassee. The tiny glass front building across from the grocery store was a post office. The largest buildings were built in the twenties or earlier and had their original tin roofs. There were two small gas stations on the highway before the curve. All businesses in the area were locally owned. Let me take you on a tour of the town from that period.

In 1975 as we approach Sopchoppy from the east, coming from Medart, you pass Crum's seafood and after that there is a small gas station on the left side of the road. It has a tall overhang and a single round-cornered, tall gas pump. The station is owned and operated by Laurice Roberts. His only employee and mechanic's name is Johnny B. Johnny B works in the open-air service bay attached to the station. He'll pause and pump your gas when you drive over the rubber hose, and a bell rings.

There is a wooden bench outside in front of the plate glass window, under the gas pump's carport. Inside the store there is a small assortment of oil, snacks, and other items you might need when traveling. Mister Laurice would go to town on Monday's, buying items at K-mart. He'd then resell them in his station for a little bit more. The K-mart price tags would still be visible on the merchandise.

Now we'll travel closer to town, past Roddenberry Realty. There is another gas station called Evan's on the right. This station has two square gas pumps, a very tiny shade overhead structure and a small store behind them. Carlton Evans owned the store, and it carried items needed for fishing in the area. You could find a broad selection of cane poles, Zebco rod-n-reels, small tackle, and live bait.

When I say good selection, I mean more than one pole. There were usually a dozen cane poles and two spinning rods outfitted with a Zebco 33 or 202. Your choice of live bait was crickets and earthworms. Evan's bought worms too, but more about that later.

Now we are at the sharp banked curve on Highway 319 that will take you away from the town. Follow the curve and you are on your way to Carrabelle, go straight and you are in Sopchoppy. At the "Y" of this intersection is the "new" at that time Gulf gas station – which is now an Express Lane. You need to be careful exiting the 20-degree banked curve, transitioning onto Sopchoppy's flat main road.

We'll go straight, off the highway onto the road that leads "in" to Sopchoppy's downtown. The road is not smooth black asphalt like Highway 319. This is coarse, rough pavement made from crushed oyster shells. The road looks like they made it by pouring tar over jagged gravel, now aged gray with white beach sand filling its crevices. On either side of the road are shallow sand-filled gullies, broken concrete sidewalks, and large live oak trees in the vacant lots.

The first building on the right is the old "Cracker" house with a twin gable roof that you can barely see. A cracker-style house is old Florida architecture style like a "Shotgun". It had a hallway in the middle of the home; you could shoot a shotgun through it and hit the back door. There are only two rooms on either side of the hallway, in the corners. This house was once the biggest home in the town.

One of my grandfather's best friends, Ed Lawhon, used to live in this old house. My grandfather helped take care of him and would drive him around. They sat together on the Loafer's Bench. After Mr. Lawhon left the house to my granddaddy years later, my dad took me inside. It was like a time-capsule with cans and appliances from the 1930's. The cloth wiring and ceramic insulators were nailed to the interior walls.

Next, we approach downtown. On the right is an old train depot. The train tracks were removed in 1946. My dad says there used to be a movie house here, although I'm not sure that means the same thing in this day and time.

After the depot, on the right, is a small storefront. It is a wooden building with a tin-covered gable roof having a short overhang facing the road. Large wood-framed, wavy plate glass windows are on either side of the entry. The large stone slab step would take you into the store if it were open. This used to be the primary sundry store of Sopchoppy. Now it is home to a large wooden slat bench that can seat four adults. The building's overhang gave the bench shade half of the day. The bench is fondly known as the "Loafer's Bench".

The Loafer's Bench is a landmark in Sopchoppy. My granddaddy would stop here after leaving Laurice's gas station. Mema would judge how well grandaddy had progressed in his day by asking if he was at the Loafer's Bench or still at Laurice's. He and his friends would sit there for hours, discussing everything important and keeping a watchful eye on the Sopchoppy traffic.

"George, have you ever seen a day as hot as this one?", his friend John Pigott would ask.

"Nope... I ain't never seen a day as hot as this." My granddaddy replied.

The next day...

"*George, have you ever heard a rain as hard as last night?"*

"Nope... I ain't never heard a rain such as last night."

These were the important topics discussed at the Loafers Bench.

Awkwardly, the bench received notoriety when a liberal theater student named Bill Gwynn from Florida State University passed through town. Mr. Gwynn was a self-proclaimed creative writer and told them he was writing a book about the area that would include poetry.

He asked to sit on the bench with Granddaddy and his friends. Later, when asked about the meeting, my granddaddy said Mr. Gwynn was "crazy" and told wild stories.

The visitor asked if a picture could be taken of him talking to my granddaddy and all his friends. They didn't think anything of it.

Several months later, in January 1976, my aunts noticed a book display at a bookstore in the Tallahassee Mall. Stacks of books, arranged in a pyramid display, had a sienna-tinted picture of my granddaddy and his friends sitting on the Loafer's Bench. The author, wearing a large cowboy hat, was sitting with them, arms outstretched telling a tall tale. They rushed to the display to see the book. The title of the book was "Loafer's Bench". Their jaws dropped after picking up the book and looking at the back cover.

On the opposite side, upside down, was a picture of the author running naked in woods! with the title "The Man Who Lives Inside Me". Gasp!

"What is this!", my Aunt Nena cried.

My Aunt Sarah laughed, and they continued to thumb through the book. Inside was poetry that didn't rhyme about the author's body parts and creative thoughts. The writings did not fit in with Sopchoppy at all! My aunts bought two copies of the book. They couldn't wait to show the book to Mema and Granddaddy. The bookstore put the books in a flat plain brown paper sack.

Word got around. For the next few weeks, people would come by my granddaddy's house and ask to see the book with him on the cover. My Mema would pull out the paper sack and slowly slide the book out of it and show the cover with my granddaddy on it.

"What's on the other side?" The guest would ask knowingly.

My Mema would flip over the book, and everyone would laugh at the picture of the naked man running in the woods.

"That man was crazy!" my granddaddy would exclaim, shaking his head.

The "Loafer's Bench" tradition in Sopchoppy continued. For a time, there were still references made to the "naked man book" when driving by, but the day-to-day conversations at the bench didn't change much.

"George, ever seen the wind blow like it did yesterday?"

"Nope, I ain't never seen the wind blow like that."

After passing the Loafer's Bench, we are now at the main intersection of Sopchoppy – in the '70s it was only a two-stop intersection. On the northwest corner of the intersection is the Sopchoppy Feed and Seed which has screen door entrances from either street. The feed store has a tall gabled tin roof, 80-percent of it covered in rust. This store was vacant for a long time until my dad opened the Feed Store with his fraternity brother Ronald Langston.

Ronald owned the building and the adjacent Sopchoppy Grocery, then called Langston's Dixie Dandy. Their slogan was "Where shopping is a pleasure" coincidently, the same slogan as Florida's mega-grocery chain Publix. Ronald took over the store from his father, Amos Langston. Mr. Amos always had a handful of M&Ms for the children when they came into the store. He always asked me what my Granddaddy was doing that day.

The grocery store is very small by today's standards. A couple of Coke machines are in front of the store, blocking its windows. The parts of windows you can see have poster board signs advertising pork and chicken prices.

Inside, the grocery store has a low ceiling. Tall, deep metal shelves run to the back of the store. This is the coldest building in Sopchoppy. You came inside just to get a break from the heat. In the back is the butcher shop run by Dickie. He had a wood paneling wall between the meat counter and cutting room/freezer.

Typical to most grocery stores, the produce was on the far right, and the milk/dairy was on the far left. I think in those days it had more to do with where the electricity was versus trying to make you take a trip around the whole store. This store could be walked though in just a few minutes. The entrance door rings a bell every time it is opened.

Right at the entrance are two cash registers with wide belts to move groceries along. Sopchoppy is one of few places I've been where you could buy things on credit – before credit cards existed. You could just say, "put it on my tab". Everyone in town had a "tab" with the grocery store. At the end of the month, Ronald would send a bill to all the families in Sopchoppy.

Remarkably, the cashiers would know whose account to debit. There were several common surnames in Sopchoppy with the last name of Langston, Evans, Strickland and Crum. Any member of a household could charge something against their family's account. The city of Sopchoppy had an account, with multiple employees charging. I don't know how the cashiers kept all the accounts correct.

In the back left of the store, elevated, was Ronald's office. From here he had a vantage point that overlooked the entire store. Every evening when we drove past the store, if the lights were on in the back, my dad would say "Ronald's in there counting his money". Though in reality, Ronald was probably trying to figure out how to make ends meet in such a small town with so many credit accounts.

On the southeast corner of the main intersection, before the grocery store, is an old boarding house that extends down the street, with a long porch facing north. The primary entrance is on the main road. I never had a reason to go there. My uncle Dan said at one time it was a Ford dealership, which is hard to believe.

A block and half south of the boarding house was my great grandmother's house. Grandma Kemp lived in a small brick ranch house with a single car carport and attached screened porch. She had large fig trees in her backyard, and we had to have fig preserves whenever we visited her house. She lived with my Aunt Clara who was never married. Aunt Clara was well known for her knowledge of the Bible and was sought out for cross-referencing scriptures in books. My biggest memory of Grandma Kemp's house was the large black bear head that was mounted and kept in Uncle Bernies old room.

I remember my dad asking Grandma Kemp how it felt to be 100 years old at the large family celebration of her birthday.

"'Bout like 99." was Grandma Kemp's reply with a big smile.

Further east on the main road, across from Langston's grocery store, is the post office. Then, the newest building in town, made of red-colored brick laid in a stacked pattern surrounding two large plate glass windows. Almost all the other buildings in town were wooden, built off the ground, with white clapboard, wood plank flooring and tin roofs. Ronald's store and the post office were at ground level with terrazzo floors. The post office has a small concrete slab in front, with a large familiar blue mailbox.

Just inside the post office's swinging glass doors is narrow room lined from top to bottom with post office boxes. Each box with its own tiny square steel door, even tinier window, lock and a number. The post office boxes could be seen from the outside, through the large glass windows.

To the left of this room, behind another door, is where Maj Strickland, the post mistress works. She's behind the counter to manage any packages that won't fit in the box and sells stamps. Maj put the mail in the boxes each morning. Of course, she knew every person's name that entered the door. If you were looking for someone, just ask Maj if they have been by the post office yet. She would give you an idea on which way they were headed.

There is no marked parking in the town of Sopchoppy. If you are going to post office or the grocery store, you just pulled up beside it. In a larger town, you might call it parallel parking, but that would imply squeezing in between two cars with an artful steering maneuver. Nope, not in Sopchoppy. You just pull up next to the store. In the rare occasion that there was more than one car parked, you would wait in the road for someone to leave or just block the road for a short spell.

For a time, the town had a police officer named Claxton Vause. He happened to also be my Sunday school teacher. Claxton would let us drive a car in Sopchoppy, well before we were 16 years old and had a driver's license. We had to be able to see over the steering wheel and reach the gas and brake pedals. It was okay to sit on a pillow. We also had to stay in town or on unpaved roads. If we crossed the highway or if he caught us driving crazy, Claxton would pull us over and recite Bible verses for what seemed like hours. He would also tell our parents.

My cousin Brad, also underage for driving, once drove across the highway to visit the Junior Food Store, which was just past the Gulf station on Highway 319. He did not escape Claxton's watchful eye. We all learned from his mistake.

On either side of the main street, blocks are laid out in a grid pattern. The streets used to be numbered 1st, 2nd, 3rd and so on. While I lived there, they changed the street names to proper names like Rose Steet, Municipal Avenue,

Yellowjacket Road and Faith Avenue. My dad said this was because of a new state emergency management mandate.

The city council had little time to come up with names, but all had meaning behind them. Calling the main road through Sopchoppy "Rose Street" instead of "Main Street" was the most controversial choice.

"There aren't any damn roses on that street", I heard my dad say more than once.

Municipal Avenue has all the city-owned buildings on it and the water tower. Faith Avenue has the Sopchoppy First Baptist Church and the Methodist Church on either side. At the end of Yellowjacket Road is the Sopchoppy High School and old gymnasium. These buildings were made from solid coquina stones and wooden framed windows and doors.

A yellowjacket wasp was the Sopchoppy school mascot. My dad and all his friends went to school there, from kindergarten through 12th grade. It was an elementary school when I lived in Sopchoppy. My grandmother worked in the cafeteria. In the 70's, the old historic gym was run down, and its wooden gym floors had holes in it. The stone's mortar was partially covered with black mold and the mold dripped down from the top coping stone like licorice icing poured on top of a cake.

Past the Dixie Dandy on the right, a two-story white building sits back from Rose Street. This is where the Lions Club meets. My grandfather was a member of the Lions Club, and they met every Thursday. Their mission was to raise money to help the visually impaired, but everyone in

Sopchoppy knew them for their calendars. The calendars simply have an updated picture of all the club members surrounded by advertisements from local businesses.

What made the calendar special was that the tear off paper months had nearly all Lions Club family members significant day(s) documented. The names with birthdays or anniversaries are printed inside the square for each day. If the person was deceased, a cross is next to their name.

Members of the Lions Club were the patriarchs of nearly every major family in Sopchoppy. So, this meant they created a birthday calendar for nearly the entire town!

Driving past the Lions Club, at the end of Yellowjacket Road is my dad's friend's house, his friend's name is Bully. He lived in Thomasville, Georgia, but came back to his hometown in Sopchoppy on weekends... until he moved there permanently after retiring from road work.

There's a story related to Bully that explains what kind of town Sopchoppy was. Bully's television stopped working. It was old. He thought it would cost too much to fix and decided it was time to part with it. Bully took the television to the city dump.

The dump wasn't too far from his house. The dump was a cleared-out field surrounded by woods with a big heap of dirt pushed up behind a pile of trash. Bully put the television on the tailgate of his truck, drove it to the dump and then set it down at the edge of the trash pile.

Televisions were heavy then, large weighty boxes with a thick glass screen. They were filled with glass tubes and copper wire, so you didn't just throw a TV out of the truck. You had to put your back into it and wrap your arms around the box. You gently put the TV on the ground. If you dropped it the glass screen would shatter, leaving dangerous shards for someone to step on.

At that time, televisions could still be repaired. It wasn't a cheap or quick process, but it could be done. My Uncle Buddy learned how to fix TVs. He bought specialized repair equipment and practiced on friends and relatives' televisions. Buddy had dozens of old televisions in various states of repair.

Because of the time involved in fixing a TV, the standard procedure was for Buddy to bring one of his TVs and set it on your broken TV. You watched the loaner TV until Buddy had time to look at yours or get the parts. There were a lot of people in Sopchoppy that had somewhat "portable" TV's sitting on top of their wooden console television sets, waiting for Buddy to get around to fixing.

Bully's TV repair case was different. Soon after Bully dropped off his broken television at the dump, my uncle Buddy was dropping off his trash. He saw the TV and recognized it as being Bully's. Buddy took the TV home and worked on it over the next few weeks. When he was finished, he took the television back to Bully's house and carefully placed the TV on the front porch. He left without knocking or saying a word.

"Bully, I thought you threw that old broken TV away?" Bully's wife Arie came into the house saying,

"I did", Bully replied, walking to the porch.

There it was - the same television that Bully took to the dump just three weeks prior. Thinking that something must be up, Bully plugged in the TV and turned it on. It worked! He just shook his head.

As you continue driving on Rose Street, heading out of town towards the Apalachicola National Forest, you will reach another fork in the road. Two bridges cross the Sopchoppy River. The town of Sopchoppy was named after the Sopchoppy River.

The historians say the word Sopchoppy was a Spanish interpretation or corruption of the Muskogee Indian word "Lokchapi". Which is composed of the Indian words for red oak and stem. Others say the word came from the words SOKHE and CHAPKE meaning "long twisting river". Regardless, the Spanish named it as the Rio Chachave. In 1894 the CT&G (Carrabelle, Tallahassee & Georgia) railroad set up the town where it is today and called it Sopchoppy. People today are still having trouble saying its name or believing it's a real word.

The bridge on the left, going straight, is on State Road 22. The bridge was built in 1968 on concrete pilings to modern standards. It has wide shoulders on either side of the road. This road was going to be the shortcut to Panama

City. It was going to take you away from the scenic route of Highway 98, which was built right on the edge of the Gulf of Mexico, going through fishing villages like Carrabelle, Apalachicola, and Cape San Blas.

State Road 22 goes through my granddaddy's land, and he provided a borrow pit for them to build the road. It goes past the cemetery where the original town of Sopchoppy used to be before the railroad. The road only goes another 7 miles after that.

It seems that the swamp approaching Tate's Hell was a little more difficult to build a road on than the State of Florida expected, so the highway project was abandoned. The "good" bridge on State Road 22 essentially goes nowhere, unless you want to take a short cut to the town cemetery.

The older trestle bridge on the right was built in 1940 on wood pilings. It is extremely narrow by today's standards. The concrete picket guard rails are only about 18-inches high. Nearly everyone straddles the centerline when going over this bridge. Bully said it was made only for Volkswagen Beetles.

This bridge takes you on Smith Creek Highway, through the land the Langston family owns. It continues through the National Forest into Gadsden County. Just after the bridge is my Mema and Grandaddy's house. A little after that is the entrance to Indian Summer.

The old bridge reminds me of another typical Sopchoppy story...

My grandmother, I called her Mema, lived to be 103-years old. She was healthy and in good spirits until the day she died. Mema had two childhood friends attend her 100th birthday party that were both older than her. The three of them were later crowned Worm Gruntin' Queens – but more about that later.

When I tell people about my Mema's health and her friends, they ask me, "What's in the water down there in Sopchoppy?"

One of my Mema's friends, Miss Myrtle, still drove her car every day. Everyone in Sopchoppy knew her car, a large, white squared-off General Motors sedan. You would occasionally see it parked in front of the grocery store, more slanted than parallel to the road. Sometimes her car partially blocked a lane on Rose Street, the tail-end still in the road. People just casually drove around it. They knew it was Miss Mrytle.

When traveling out of Sopchoppy, toward Smith Creek Highway, a local driver might see Miss Myrtle's car coming towards the narrow bridge, her gray beehive hairdo standing tall behind the steering wheel. Caution was needed. It was better to just slow down and pull off the side of the road before the bridge. Give Mrs. Myrtle the space she needs for crossing. She was entitled to it. You exchange a friendly wave as Miss Myrtle passes you, going towards town. Now you can get back on the road and safely cross the bridge.

My parents' names are George Ed and Sandra and as early as I can remember, they took me to Sopchoppy. We lived in Tallahassee where my dad was an accountant. It was given that every weekend we were going to make the 35-mile drive to this small little town.

My first memory of being around Sopchoppy is going hunting with my dad. I was probably six years old. We took his black Volkswagen Beetle into the woods with his good friend Bobby Jack. Bobby Jack was from Sopchoppy also and he convinced my dad to go to college. My dad said there was no school application process, they just went up to the counter and signed up on the same day. They both graduated from Florida State University.

Dad and Bobby Jack sat in front of the Volkswagen with their shotguns and Bo Jack sat in the back with me. Obviously, Bo Jack is Bobby Jack's son. We rode all day, on all the fire roads of the Apalachicola National Forest, trying to find dogs barking. Hunters used dogs to track and chase deer. After driving what seemed like forever, we'd suddenly stop.

"George, I think I hear them dogs" Bobby Jack would tell my dad.

"I don't hear 'em." was my dad's response

We'd sit for five minutes, then the dogs' barking pitch would get higher.

"Now I hear 'em!" Dad confirmed for all of us.

We then drove around in the woods some more. Dad and Bobby Jack listening to dogs barking at each stop, trying to figure out which way the dogs were going and what road they might cross. You couldn't hear the dogs over the rumble of the Volkswagen's rear engine. Bo Jack and I knew we had to be quiet when the engine stopped.

At some point, we'd lose track of the dogs and Dad would pull out cans of Dinty Moore Beef Stew. He had them sitting on top of the car's engine, heating up. It was lunch time. Bo Jack and I had warm beef stew. Dad and Bobby Jack ate sardines on Saltine crackers.

We went "deer hunting" on many fall Saturdays. In all those times, I never saw my dad shoot his gun. He finally confessed to me when I was an adult that he never wanted to kill a deer. He just liked riding in the woods with Bobby Jack and listening to the dogs' bark.

In Tallahassee, I had two relatives on my mom's side, Grandaddy Scott and my grandmother Garnet. I barely remember my grandmother Garnet, who passed away when I was three years old. After she died, my Granddaddy Scott came to live with us. He was in his fifties when my mom was born, and she was their only child.

Nearly all my dad's family lived in Sopchoppy. Here lived my Granddaddy Strickland and Mema. Five of my dad's adult siblings lived in Sopchoppy. I had a half-dozen cousins that were close to my age – and that was growing. There were many family dinners or fish fries and my Sopchoppy grandparent's house seemed to have a whirlwind of activity.

Uncles, aunts, cousins, family friends passed through my grandparents' house at all times of the day. They would come in, share a quick story, eat a bite of cake, leave (or take) vegetables on top of the chest freezer and be gone ten minutes later. Sopchoppy was busy compared to our life in Tallahassee, which was constituted of my dad working, elementary school and sporadic visits to my parent's friends.

We traveled back and forth to Sopchoppy in my dad's 1964½ Ford Mustang. He bought the car in July of 1964, several months before I was born. If you didn't know, there was a lot of buzz about the Mustang prior to its release. The car was essentially a re-skinned Ford Falcon, but the lines of the Mustang were sleek and modern. My dad bought the car from his uncle's Ford dealership in Quincy. He custom ordered the Mustang coupe, without having seen the actual car.

"The Mustang" was Prairie Bronze with Palomino interior. My dad selected almost every option when ordering the car. The pony car had a 260-cubic-inch V8 engine (my dad thought a 289 would be too much). The 260-engine option wasn't available after 1964. It had automatic transmission, air conditioning and a center console between the two low-backed bucket seats. The only options left off were power brakes, power steering and rear seat belts. My dad thought the car would be too small to need power-assisted driving.

Mom has told me the story about taking me to see my Mema and Granddaddy soon after I was born. I was their first grandson with the last name Strickland, and they gave me the name "George" after my granddaddy. Granddaddy's name was George Hyman, dad's name was George Edwin, and my name was George Scott. My parents couldn't wait to tell my granddaddy what my name was, thinking he would be honored. Instead, he told them that every donkey and jackass from Sopchoppy to Tallahassee was named "George". From then on, I guess, I was called "Scott" or "Scotty".

I remember traveling to Sopchoppy, sitting on the center console between the front seats of the Mustang. My parents were on either side. When we first got in the car, the chrome metal console would be too hot to touch. Once underway, the under-console air conditioner worked well. The four AC vents were right in front of the console aimed directly at me.

This was a time before children rode in car seats, heck even seat belts - which then only went across your lap, weren't in fashion. My dad always had his front seat belts folded neatly on either side of the bucket seats. My crash protection was my dad's right arm preventing me from going through the windshield during emergency braking. During one rapid stop, my body slid on the chrome center console into the gear shifter, slamming the transmission into park. My dad said the car always shifted rougher after that incident.

After years of traveling back and forth every weekend, my dad had an opportunity to buy land in Sopchoppy. Property lots were going on sale in a new development called Indian Summer. Roads had been carved out of woods in the land across from my grandparents' house. There were parcels of land going on sale, even on the river. Keeping in theme with the development's name, the roads were named after Indian tribes: Seminole, Cherokee, Blackhawk for example.

My dad and Uncle Bernie scouted the newly surveyed area and came to purchase the two highest elevation river parcels within the development. This was important because the Sopchoppy River was prone to flooding if a storm system dumped 10-inches or more of rain. This land purchase cemented our connection with Sopchoppy.

With money borrowed from my Granddaddy Scott, mom and dad bought a used two-bedroom, single-wide trailer for their new river lot. We now had a place to stay in Sopchoppy! My granddaddy Scott came along with us and slept on the couch. His snoring was notoriously loud, and it shook the walls of the trailer.

Being in Sopchoppy overnight, it afforded us the time to go fishing in the mornings with my dad's friend Bully. I was able to spend more time with my cousins Brad and David. To quote Shakespeare, these were the "Salad days" of my youth.

I remember moving from playing T-ball to little league baseball, while living in Tallahassee. T-ball was fun! Everybody got to hit the ball! However, in little league baseball, a batter was often hit by the inexperienced pitcher practicing his curve ball for the first time. After taking three errant thrown balls into my thigh and arm, my nervousness increased, and my batting ability progressively decreased.

"Step in front of the ball!" my hack coaches were telling me.

They were there to win at all costs and would say anything to get me on base. During one practice I finally worked up the courage to ask my dad.

"Dad, do you enjoy baseball?" was how I started.

"Why son? Don't you?" He responded.

"It's okay, I guess. Wouldn't you have more fun if we went fishing?" I tried to reason.

My dad could not have agreed more. He got a big smile on his face. He talked with the coach, we got into the Mustang, and we headed to Sopchoppy. I never played baseball again. Instead, we resumed spending our full weekends in Sopchoppy.

One week my dad and I went to the trailer in Sopchoppy early. It had been raining all week and Dad wanted to check on the property. When we arrived, we saw the river water, well outside of the banks. It had crept over ten feet closer to the trailer. Instead of a slow meandering tidal flow, the river's black water rushed looking like Coca-Cola coming out of fountain. The water was still a hundred feet from the trailer, which was elevated thirty feet above the banks.

My dad hammered a stake at the water's edge. We began moving lawn furniture and the grill out of the yard. A few hours later, the wooden stake planted by my father was almost under water. It was still raining. My dad waded into water and moved the stake to the new water line.

My mom and younger sister Stacey came later in the early evening. The water was now within 10 feet of the trailer. My dad was becoming more nervous about the situation. My uncles came over with concrete blocks. Working with my dad, they lifted the trailer's furniture on top of the blocks to provide greater elevation between our belongings and the river. I went home with my mom and sister. My dad stayed to check the rising water through the entire night.

The next day, we returned and parked in the vacant lot across from my family's trailer. Water surrounded the trailer and flowed underneath, between its concrete block foundation. My dad waded through the water to meet us.

"I think the water's starting to recede!" my dad exclaimed with relief.

My dad and Uncle Bernie had scouted well. Every river lot in Indian Summer was under five or more feet of water except for the two they had bought. My sister and I played in the cresting water around the trailer, well away from the strong flow near the river's original banks. This was a surreal experience swimming in the front yard.

We marveled at the colonies of ants climbing on top of each other. They were fighting for survival, using each other to try to stay afloat. Cousins came over and I retrieved my Styrofoam surfboard. We floated on the surfboard and inflatable plastic ring toys, playing in the water all day. Family members and friends came by to marvel at the flooding event.

My parents divorced when I was eleven. When you're at that age there is no complete understanding of what is happening to your family. My knowledge of divorce was limited to the knowledge gained by hearing Tammy Wynette songs played on the Tampa AM station Sun Country. It was the only radio station that came in clearly in Sopchoppy.

My mom was now alone, my Granddaddy Scott living with us downstairs. I remember the house being quiet without my parents yelling. Now I go to Sopchoppy on weekends with my dad, without my mom. She later told me how difficult it was not to see Mema and Granddaddy anymore.

My mom quickly re-married, to a car salesman she recently met named Russell. Shortly after, my dad married Leona who had two daughters named Tannye and Beth. My sister Stacey and I were at both weddings. For a short time, Russell and my mom moved us to Quincy Florida, which is still only an hour's drive from Sopchoppy.

Soon after that though, Russell was offered the opportunity of a lifetime for a car salesman. He bought the Ford dealership in his hometown of Berea Kentucky. We were moving a second time, this time far away.

That is how I came to live in Sopchoppy only during the hot summer months between 1976 and 1981. I lived with my dad, stepmother, sister and two stepsisters in Indian Summer on the Sopchoppy river. The rest of the year, my sister Stacey and I lived in Berea, Kentucky with my mom and stepfather. I now lived and went to high school in a town that was an 11 hours' drive from north Florida.

Fortunately, my mom and dad were on good enough terms to make this arrangement work. I think the yearly separation I had with Sopchoppy gave me a different perspective on the town. During the summer, school was out, I was away from my school friends, and there was plenty of free time. I had many relatives there, where I had none in Berea. I could see that Sopchoppy was not "normal". Berea was a small town with Population of 16,000. That was a metropolis compared to tiny Sopchoppy – Population 450.

Being there primarily in the summers, it was always hot when I lived in Sopchoppy. The internet did not exist. Cell phones did not exist. Steve Jobs had just released the first apple computer. It wasn't until 1980 that we had an Atari game console. My dad and stepmother worked full-time in Tallahassee, Florida – working for the State of Florida. They were gone from 6:30 AM to 6:00 PM.

That left me and my sisters alone in Sopchoppy to fill our days with chores, swimming in the river, scheming with cousins, visiting Mema, and later for me – working in the Sopchoppy Feed & Seed. They were simple times, I guess.

I wanted to capture the stories that I remember about Sopchoppy. If for no one else, then for my grandchildren. Many of my friends and family have heard these stories before. A few of the stories I've never told. Times have changed in the fifty years since I lived in Sopchoppy. Sopchoppy, not so much.

The memories of a teenager – the memories now misty being nearly fifty years old - are probably not the most reliable source. The stories are as true and real as the memories of a 13-year-old boy can be. I'm sorry if I get a name wrong. I don't intend to embarrass anyone.

Teenagers can be as cruel as the hot summer months of north Florida. It is said that necessity is the mother of invention – I can attest that boredom is the mother of mischievousness.

Mema and Granddaddy

To me, everything in Sopchoppy revolved around my Mema and Granddaddy's house. It was a daily stopping place for my aunts, uncles, and cousins. It was a place for good food, fellowship and catching up on the happenings in Sopchoppy. Their house was the Strickland family hub for decades, until my grandmother passed.

Their house was just outside of the Sopchoppy city limits, across the river on your way to Smith Creek. It was on the left, just before Indian Summer. The split-level home was set back from the road at the end of a long narrow dirt lane. On either side of the lane was a large Bahia-grass covered lawn, usually cut very short, and huge azalea bushes. Looking to the right of the house was a large cattle gate leading into the cow pasture. A small corn crib barn sits in the middle of the pasture. My granddaddy used to keep a blonde horse named Prince here.

I remember seeing John Pigott run over Mema's peacock on their driveway. He never saw the bird. He could barely see enough to drive. When I was young, that peacock was almost as tall as I was. Its tail feathers spread out were wider than my arm span. I was traumatized by the driveway incident. Mema just shrugged it off because she didn't miss the noise of the frequent peacock calls.

Mema and Grandaddy's house is brick with wood siding on the second floor. The second story was on the right with an entrance off the large brick patio. The patio is surrounded by a foot and half brick wall. This was the primary entrance used by everyone. There is also a double entry door that entered the foyer, towards the main part of the house, but I don't remember anyone ever using that entrance.

The patio entry had a large, wood-frame screen door with a long extension spring keeping it closed. When you entered the door and stepped inside, the door would slam, hitting the door frame with a loud "thwack". At this time, you would usually announce your entry by yelling "Anybody home?"

"Yeah, come on in the house", my Granddaddy would answer back.

An enclosed sunken porch with a brick floor is just inside with a couch and a chair. An old out-of-tune, upright piano is in the back corner. This is where Mema would play and sing "Froggy went a-courtin'" and other songs to her grand kids.

Frog went a-courtin', and he did ride, Uh-huh,
Frog went a-courtin', and he did ride, Uh-huh,
Frog went a-courtin', and he did ride.
With a sword and a pistol by his side, Uh-huh.

Straight is a narrow hallway leading to the back porch, this is where Granddaddy hangs his hat. It's the hall where my cousins and I would retreat to when we were in trouble or planning our next scheme against my sisters.

Steep stairs go up to a bedroom upstairs and tens of grandchildren slid down or played with a Slinky Spring toy on them. To your left is a narrow laundry room leading into the kitchen. The washing machine usually has a sack of vegetables sitting on it, brought by a relative or friend. You step up into the galley kitchen on the left, covered with a linoleum floor. The electric stove on right has something cooking on it. Depending on the day, it would be green beans for dinner or homemade chocolate syrup for ice cream.

The tiny kitchen has a U-shaped layout of wood lower cabinets, they have smooth flat doors. On the left, there are matching upper cabinets. In the middle is a white porcelain sink with clean dishes stacked on the right. A wide window with aluminum-framed glass squares overlooks hydrangeas in the front yard. The thin metal-banded Formica counter has tiny multi-color flower burst pattern. On the left counter is the stainless-steel coffee percolator. On the right counter is a homemade cake on display, sitting on a raised glass platter and covered with a glass dome.

Your eyes are drawn to the cake at once when you walk into the kitchen. It's usually pound cake, but if you're lucky, it could be a seven-layer chocolate cake or covered with penuche icing. Penuche icing is a caramel sugar that is literally poured on top of the cake. You hope that no one has scooped out the inch-thick icing layer in the hole in the middle of the cake.

Just on the other side of the counter is a small round breakfast table with four armless chairs around it. The chairs and table are tubular steel, like what you might find in a 1950's ice cream store. The wall opposite the window has a stove, refrigerator and next to that is a stacked stone wall made from pink marble with white flecks. On the other side of the stone wall is a fireplace made of the same material. The wall is jagged with each stone at a random angle. The wood paneled wall on the far side of the breakfast nook has a door opening into the foyer, a Lions Club calendar hangs on the wall.

If you come any time before 8 AM, this is where you will find my Mema and Grandaddy. My grandfather's name was George, like me and my dad. My grandmother's name was Eloise. Usually, my uncle Bernie would be sitting with them at the breakfast table drinking a cup of coffee. Uncle Bernie was what everyone called him; he was my Mema's younger brother, was a Tallahassee firefighter and retired as captain. Uncle Bernie worked with Granddaddy tending to honeybees. Together, they formed the S&K Honey Company, which was in business for many years.

"Hey Scotty, how you doin'?", my granddaddy would always ask. "Want some cake?"

Now when my Granddaddy (or anybody raised in Sopchoppy) said "want", instead of using an AH sound, he used an OH – like in the word NO. So, when he asked me if I wanted any cake it sounded like "Won't Sum?". The N and the T were almost silent.

My granddaddy was a big man, at least to my 13-year-old eyes he was. To other adults, and looking back on it today, he wasn't that big in stature - but he had a presence. People listened to him, respected him and wanted to be around him. He was built kind of like Jackie Gleason, from the old television show, The Honeymooners. He was well fed by my grandmother. He had a barrel chest with slumped shoulders. His head was big and round and mostly bald. His ears seemed bigger, taller, than they should have been. My aunts and Mema would joke about granddaddy's "big ears" and "fat fingers", but never in a demeaning way. Granddaddy joked about them as well. Somebody once said shaking hands with my granddaddy was like grabbing hold of a well-worn catcher's mitt. That's a pretty good description.

My grandaddy's hands were calloused and worn from 60 or more years of working in the woods and on the farm. His hands and arms were sun-weathered and bear the scars of thousands of bee bites. Granddaddy had the kindest, most genuine smile of anyone I have ever met. He always had a smile on his face except when someone was talking – then he would be focused on the person speaking, mouthing the words as they were saying them as if to hear them better.

Except for Sunday and attending church, my grandaddy wore a pair of cotton work trousers, usually blue, and a pressed, white short-sleeved collared shirt with a sleeveless undershirt. For church he always wore a suit and tie. Whenever he left the house, he was wearing his gray fedora, which had a black band. You never saw him outside without his hat on. If he was working on the farm in the fall and winter, fixing fences, feeding cows or driving the tractor, he would have on a pair of coveralls. When he was tending to bees in the summer, he would put on a white apron that went almost to his knees.

I remember when I was a kid, picking my granddaddy's hat up off the floor after it fell off the wall in the hallway. When I went to re-hang it, I smelled the inside of his hat. I know, that sounds weird. The inside of his hat had a sweet smell, more so than musk, it was almost like smelling the excess beeswax he harvested from the hives. Sometimes, after working hard all day, I smell the same smell inside my baseball caps.

Mema was much smaller than granddaddy. She was a beautiful lady, and her silver hair was always "fixed", meaning well-styled. Her facial features were like a southern version of Queen Elizabeth or the fictional Betty Crocker character. She had prominent cheek bones, and milky pale skin that wasn't tan like my grandfather's, even though it was wrinkled from age. She wore oval-shaped, clear-framed eyeglasses that had bi-focal lenses. She also always wore lipstick and always had a smile, but she could be stern when needed. She worked in the lunchroom and library at the Sopchoppy Elementary School, so she wouldn't take any rowdiness. Most grandkids were well aware of this, so she rarely had to raise her voice.

My grandmother had a faint Tennessee accent and told stories better than anyone. Her stories came from her life and were about her family. Her father was a doctor, who moved his family to Sopchoppy after losing everything in Miami after a hurricane. She told stories about how she and my granddaddy met. How they spent their honeymoon in the loft of an old barn, deep in the woods. How her father had birthed nearly every child in Sopchoppy.

Mema often told us how she lost her brother Bruce in a plane crash in the Rocky Mountains. He was on a plane of returning troops, coming home from the Korean war. The veterans were on the plane based on their last name's placement in the alphabet. Forty people died when their C-46 Air Transport iced over and couldn't climb the mountain. Snow and ice prevented access to the wreckage until June. Mema's stories were always detailed and colorful. They were meaningful to her, and to us. She wanted to pass them down.

"Sweet" is the word most used to describe my grandparents. They were always pleasant and generous. I remember celebrating their 50th wedding anniversary when I was a teenager. I don't ever remember a cross word between the two of them. The sternest words that came from my grandmother towards my granddaddy were, "George, now don't you be late for supper."

Now that I'm older, I know they probably weren't always this calm and settled. You can't raise seven children in a small town and not have strong will and discipline. My dad would tell me about getting in trouble after shooting out his father's truck window with a BB gun. My granddaddy was in the truck at the time, driving away after scolding my dad. My dad still remembered the beating he received afterward. My dad told me he was always getting in trouble with his good friend and his neighbor Lynn Hodge.

Dad was in the ATO fraternity at Florida State and sometimes he would share stories about their rowdiness. He told me about their pranks against rival fraternities. I think my dad and Granddaddy had their share of run-ins over my dad's behavior. My uncle Dan claimed to have saved dad from dozens of fights in high school. Uncle Dan was six inches taller, 100 pounds heavier and played linebacker for Florida State. Just Uncle Dan's presence could rescue my dad from the trouble his "hot head" got him into. My uncle Dan was a calm man and my dad looked up to his older brother.

I think my dad was a little different than the rest of Granddaddy's children. He may have been a little more challenging. My dad might drink alcohol, where they didn't. He might have a cigarette or say a cussword, and they never did. He might miss a Sunday in church on days most of his siblings made the effort.

Often at Mema's, I'd hear my Aunt Nena warn my cousins, "I don't want to hear you talkin' like your Uncle George Ed!"

According to the 1950s census, my grandparents George and Eloise had five kids: Dan 15, George 13, Jo Ann 9, Sarah 4, and Clara (Nena) 2. They lived on 2nd Street in the middle of Sopchoppy. Later, my grandparents would have two more boys, Malcom (M.O.) and Robert.

In 1950, every family patriarch of Sopchoppy lived within a few houses of each other. Family names that are very familiar in Sopchoppy: Strickland, Lawhon, Roddenberry, Roberts, Hodge, Harrell, Vause, Crum... their grandfathers and great grandfathers all lived on 1st, 2nd or 3rd street in Sopchoppy. The occupations then in Sopchoppy were mechanic, farmer, beekeeper, sawmill operator, grocery store owner. The families all lived by and depended on each other.

By the late 1970's, some of the families expanded and others contracted – while most lived in town – a few moved across the river. Sopchoppy wasn't any bigger in the late 70's than it was in the early '50's. In fact, somehow, its population was probably smaller with people now working and living in Tallahassee. The 1950 demographics and living proximity, explains how my Granddaddy (and my dad) knew everybody in Sopchoppy.

A town with one store, one deputy, one school, a loafer's bench, three churches and everyone's on a first name basis. It explains why 1970's Sopchoppy was like *The Andy Griffith Show's* fictional town of Mayberry.

I do remember getting in trouble with Mema once. She gave me her sewing shears and told me to, "go outside and cut me a switch". Never have I had a task that was so overthought. Too long and skinny and she'll have leverage, and it will sting. If it is too thick, it will be like a club and leave a bruise. Of course, a switch can't have thorns, which would be barbaric. A cattail has a weighted end with a pointed tip that might hurt more than others. If I choose something wimpy like grass, she will go find one that is worse than what I would bring in. This was a hard choice. I don't remember what I picked, and I don't remember the spanking, but I still remember looking for that switch! That was probably the point.

I've watched as my dad's personality changed over the years, so I'm sure my grandparent's temperament softened with age as his did. As kids, we were afraid of making a sound during the Florida State football games on TV, except to cheer when he did. If we did, we would be screamed at and banished to the basement for the rest of the game. Years later, his granddaughter could sing and bang on drums during the games and he would just smile at her. His now-grown children noted my dad's personality change with amazement.

I think emotions sweeten and become less strong with age, like bourbon left in barrels to endure the hot and cold seasons of numerous years. I assume, as grand kids, we were treated with patience and kindness my aunts and uncles rarely saw when they were growing up, but I could be wrong. I do know that any memories of strong discipline were long forgotten by dad when he was older. He stopped every day to see my grandmother after he retired, as did his siblings. She was showered with love and affection by her family for the last twenty years of her life. She lived to be 103 years old.

We often stopped by Mema's during breakfast. As I said before, Uncle Bernie was there every morning. Eggs, bacon and cream-of-wheat was the meal of choice – everyday. Mema would offer to scramble an egg for me, and she always served it with the cream-of-wheat poured over top. The lumpier the better. After I added a healthy dose of salt and pepper, I would eat the egg mixture and cold bacon and listen to Granddaddy, Bernie and Dad go over their daily plans. The plans could be associated with farming or tending bees. My granddaddy usually had a few dozen or more cows. He also raised watermelons, tomatoes, corn and peas – mostly for the extended family.

The 1950's census documented my grandfather's occupation as "Beekeeper" that "tends bees". For this, my grandfather was well known in the area. In fact, if you look up "Florida Beekeeping in the 1970's" a video interview with my granddaddy appears. It was filmed by the local public broadcasting station, WFSU. The full video is titled *Beekeeper.* 1970 (circa). State Archives of Florida, Florida Memory. Here is snippet of the conversation between the interviewer and my granddaddy – Granddaddy is using smoke to calm the bees and talking to the guy. Uncle Bernie is the background working with the hives. The interviewer has a quick, city-slick, reporter-like interrogational style. My grandfather speaks slow, measured and methodical.

Interviewer: *Hey - why do you have this electric fence here?*

Granddaddy: We had to put this fence here to try to keep the black bears out.

Does it, does it work?

It works, uh, it works most of the time - but if it's dry - the weather's dry and all and the bear is real hungry - he will go through it

How much honey do you lose to Bears

Every year, well uh, we lose... I wouldn't know just exactly how much -but if every time a bear breaks through... he'll tear down and destroy two or three or four hives and we have had them to tear down as many as 30 and 40 at a time in one night.

Okay how do you uh get the honey off of...you how do you use this smoke?

Well, you use this smoker to control the bees...they can't stand the smoke and you open the hive up and Smoke them a little bit and then they - uh - won't jump on you and sting you and you have to have the smoke to control them and that's the reason we use a smoker - just to control the bees.

How many hives do you have?

We have 50 hives in this apiary.

My grandfather explains how the bee smoker works. It looks like a coffee can with a funnel top and small fireplace bellows attached to the side. Every time my grandfather squeezes the bellows, large puffs of white smoke come out of the narrow opening at the top. While being interviewed, he is prying off the tops of the bee boxes, exposing the wooden racks that make up the beehive, puffing smoke all around the box. They look like a two-foot by nine-inch picture frame with bees wax for a canvas. The bees, under the influence of Granddaddy's bee smoker are drunkenly crawling all over the wax. Some of the combs have their hexagon cells filled with the sweet, delicious nectar known as Tupelo Honey. The interview continues:

You ever get stung?

Yes sir. I get stung every day.

Are you used to it? Does it bother you anymore?

No sir, I'm not used to it. It bothers me right on.

Do you get to where it doesn't hurt quite as bad?

It hurts you every time... it does me.

My grandfather then gives a taste of the honey to the interviewer, brushing a bee off his hand before passing it. Uncle Bernie continues to lift the honey-laden bee boxes off the ground and puts them on the trailer. The boxes weigh 90 pounds each. My grandfather looks for the queen bee and points out the differences between it and all the worker bees.

It's amazing that this 50-plus year-old time capsule of a video exists and that anyone can watch it on YouTube. It gives me fond memories of the humor, cadence and care with which my grandfather spoke. My time working "in the bees" was thankfully short. My uncle, Bernie and later my uncle Mo worked decades "tending bees". It's hard, sweaty work. My dad and I were occasionally enlisted for help moving bees or extracting honey.

Bees were moved in the middle of the night, when the insects were all working in their hives instead of flying around gathering pollen from the forest. My contribution to this activity, given my age and weakness, was riding in the truck with my dad, half asleep. He would wake me at Four A.M. in the morning and tell me, "It's time to move the bees"! After driving for what seemed forever in the middle of the woods (the Apalachicola National Forest), we would arrive at the apiary where wooden bee boxes are stacked four feet tall on a trailer.

Bee boxes had been stacked there the day before by my grandfather and Uncle Bernie. After they hooked up the trailer using their 12-volt flashlight for illumination, we would move the cargo of live bees to a new location. They were moved to either another fenced-in apiary in the woods or the "honey house" for extracting. Once re-located, the trailer was left for unloading the next day. We would arrive back at Mema's just at daybreak. She would have a hearty breakfast waiting on us.

"Moving Bees" was a done in spring and early summer to keep the hives in a fertile location for fresh pollen. The bees could only fly a couple of miles from the hive. They had to be moved to different locations to make the most honey. I know now how much planning and experience is involved with getting the bees in the right spot. My focus at the breakfast table was on pound cake or eggs and bacon when these important conversations were held between Granddaddy and Uncle Bernie.

"Extracting honey" was done in the hottest time of the Spring, just before Summer. The temperature in north Florida would be in the upper 90's and the humidity over 90%. Being twenty miles from the coast and surrounded by forest – there was no wind to speak of. It was almost has hot as the "dog days" of Summer and the only relief outside from heat was an afternoon thunderstorm. There was never any relief from the humidity without the miracle of air-conditioning.

Extracting honey is exactly what it sounds like. It is the process of getting the honey out of the beehives so that it can be barreled or bottled for sale. The hives are wood boxes that were either 6 or 9-1/2 inches tall. Each box holds eight or ten frames with a wax starter honeycomb for the queen bee to lay eggs. Worker bees stored pollen and honey in the wax for food. There is air space between each frame for the bees to expand and fill the hexagon-shaped wax cells. The box, or hive body, could be home for 50-60 thousand bees. The wooden boxes have a removable wood top and bottom. The bees could access the interior through small holes leading to the inside.

We would extract honey in a building my grandfather and uncle had built called "the honey house". I mean what else would you call it? The honey house was on the lot across from my dad's house in Indian Summer. Extracting honey would take many days over a couple of weeks. The honey house did not have air conditioning. There was no escape from the summer heat and humidity in this cinder-block building. There were two rooms in the honey house, one for wood working which had table saws, band saws and cabinets covered in fine sawdust. This is where my granddaddy and uncle made and repaired bee hives. The other room was for extracting honey. This room did not have sawdust, the walls were clean and white, but the floor was sticky from the residue of bees' wax and honey.

In the middle of the extracting room was a rectangular stainless-steel trough, elevated on steel legs. Later I found out this was called an "Auto Uncapper". At one end of the trough was a feeder that would receive the wooden frame that had wax cells full of honey. It stripped off the top cap of wax from the honey-filled cells. A chain conveyor in the trough would slowly move the frame with exposed honey toward the two large extractors used for slinging the honey out of the honeycomb. The uncapper was electrically heated to soften the wax on the honeycomb and frame.

So, we were working in Florida, in June, in a room with a heater. We were wearing long pants and long-sleeved shirts in this room with stinging insects willing to give up their lives to protect their honey. You can see why I didn't look forward to this time of year.

My job was using a metal scraping tool to remove the excess wax from the top and sides of the wooden frames. This allowed the frames to fit better inside the uncapper's feeder, trough and the honey extractors. The extractors were large six-foot round stainless-steel tubs with a hinged top. Inside was a round carrier for holding 30 wood-framed honeycombs. After un-capping each frame to expose the honey, my dad or uncles would load the extractor, when full they would power on the motor to spin the carrier inside the barrel. This is when I got to go outside because of the noise echoing inside the Cinder block building. Finally, a breath of the slightly cooler fresh air!

The centrifugal force generated by this motor-driven extractor did its job well. Honey was efficiently slung out of the wood frames leaving the interior walls covered in syrupy liquid. Gravity pulled the liquid into a conical base and drained it into a container. This allowed transfer to an extremely large vat at the end of the room. This large tank could hold thousands of gallons of honey. The vat would later be used to fill 55-gallon metal barrels with honey for commercial sale. The full barrels weighed more than 600 pounds each. The excess beeswax was melted and molded into 25-pound blocks. This was just as valuable as the precious honey. The wax was sold to cosmetic manufacturers and more.

These were long days, but my grandfather and uncles did the heavy lifting. Granddaddy was the only person wearing short sleeves. He moved the heavy bee boxes from a separate room persuading the bees out of the hive with a scrapper and smoker. His arms were covered with purple welts from many bee stings over many days and years. You would sometimes see a stinger or two, bee guts still attached, embedded in my grandfather's forearm.

Somehow, he was comfortable around bees, and I think the bees sensed that. He might only get stung a few times in a day, even though he is surrounded by thousands of bees for hours at a time. He would never give you any sign that he was stung. You would just see the stingers still entrenched on his arm. My dad on the other hand...

"Damn!", he would yell

We all knew when Dad had been stung. Uncle Dan didn't work with the bees because stings bothered him so much. Thankfully my extracting job was mostly separate from the bees, and I've erased any memories of getting stung. What I remember most is tasting the fresh honey after scraping it off the comb. Nothing tastes sweeter than tupelo honey with warm bits of beeswax! You understand why the bears can't resist.

The highlight of these days and weeks was dinner, which was at lunchtime for those not familiar with the southern vernacular. The meal that we ate at the end of the day was called "supper". We ate at the big table at my Mema's house. There would be bacon seasoned green field peas, creamed corn, fried chicken with rice and chicken gravy. We washed the home-grown, home-cooked meal down with an ice-cold glass of home-made sweet tea. On Sunday's we would have roast beef and rice with brown gravy. My granddaddy, before every meal, would say the following grace "Lord, bless this food and all our many blessings. In Jesus' name, Amen."

We all repeated, "Amen."

For dessert, we would get a big slice of Mema's sour cream pound cake. I liked it best if the cake "fell" while cooking, so that the consistency was dense and moist. Sometimes the pound cake would be dressed up with fresh blue berries inside or even better with the caramelized sugar icing called penuche. My Mema and all her daughters make the most incredible desserts. For potlucks or mullet fish fries, it was a common practice to choke down your food as much as possible so that you could get to the dessert table before your favorite was gone.

When the Sopchoppy Baptist Church held "dinner on the grounds" we searched for the cake carriers with "Strickland" or "Langston" written on the masking tape. Unapologetically getting dessert at the same time as your meal. If you ever come across a Sopchoppy Homemakers Cookbook, buy it! It is filled with delicious recipes from local ladies. My Mema's recipes were documented by my aunts, who followed behind her measuring the ingredients that she could gage perfectly by sight or feeling.

On Sunday mornings in Sopchoppy it was expected for you to attend church at 11:00 A.M. If you didn't go to church, then it was presumed you wouldn't be eating Mema's roast and rice. When I was younger, the church was very small with hard oaken pews and found on Faith Avenue. Me and my cousins sat in the front row next to the piano, with our feet not touching the floor. My Aunt Sarah played the piano and Uncle Bernie played the organ on the other side of the church. Aunt Sarah gave us dirty looks when we fidgeted or poked at one another. She was an excellent piano player and could manage these looks without missing a note in the song. When she finished playing, she sat with us as the sermon was given.

The preacher would begin his fire and brimstone speech, always starting slow with a quick joke. The congregation nervously laughed, knowing what was meant to come. The preacher would continue, increasingly raising his voice, following a familiar cadence, quoting different scriptures. The adults try and find the biblical reference. You hear the thin pages of Bibles violently flipped during each sermon pause. This sometimes visibly annoyed the preacher.

The preacher always finished off red-faced as if his necktie was choking him to death. He screamed about the evils of sin and our choice between Heaven and Hell. Occasionally you would catch his glare, and you knew he was speaking directly to you!

My cousins and I were too young to understand all the sermon except for its primary message to "get saved!". By the sermon's end, all I could feel was the hardness of the pews on my buttocks and the hunger pains in my stomach.

Later the church built a larger brick church next door with cushioned pews. Still later they built a larger church on a plot of my Granddaddy's land given to them by my Uncle Dan. My grandfather was a deacon of the church. Nearly all my aunts and uncles sang in the choir. My Uncle Randy, Aunt Nena's husband, was the music leader. The Stricklands always sat in the middle and back rows of the church, on the right-hand side. The Langston's sat in front of us on same side. We, and nearly everyone in the church, sat in the same pew location every Sunday. Before the service began promptly at eleven, the adults spoke and exchanged greetings and pleasantries. Myself, only attending during the summer's, I would be greeted by people whose name's I couldn't remember with a "Hey Scotty".

Every Sunday, Deacons pass out a one-page folded paper program to everyone that enters the church. We always took one, but the program was always the same: 1) Sing a hymn standing, 2) listen to church announcements, 3) sing a hymn sitting, 4) listen to the choir sing alone, 5) sing a hymn standing while the choir moves to the congregation, 6) pass the felt-lined shiny steel plates for an offering, 7) a soloist or quartet would sing special music (usually my aunts or uncle) and finally 8) the sermon and invitational. During the choir and solo music, I would watch my Granddaddy trying to mouth the words that they were singing.

When the sermon was finished, the preacher asked for those to come before him and profess their belief in Jesus and pray for their forgiveness. The paper programs were now crinkled and nervously rolled up in our hands. We all stood, nervously singing "Just as I Am" waiting for someone to take the preacher's offer and walk up and pray in his arms. If no takers, the preacher would often ask for another verse to be sung and we waited still longer, for someone to go forward. My family sang with the congregation, knowing that a pot roast was simmering at home on the stove.

Often during the "invitational", my grandfather would go to the front of the church and kneel at the steps to pray. He took as long as he needed, before finishing and returning to his seat.

On some Sunday's, the entire extended family would come to my Mema and Granddaddy's house. Grandaddy would make homemade vanilla ice cream with fresh peaches included. Others would bring their churns with another ice cream recipe. Three or four electric ice cream churns would be doing their jobs. We all impatiently waited for the churns to stop, signaling that the cream was now frozen. In the meantime, my cousins and I would contribute by re-filling the churns with ice or rock salt. The rock salt melted the ice bringing the cream's temperature below freezing, colder than ice alone. Occasionally we put a salt-covered piece of ice in our mouths, waiting for ice cream. We finally ate the ice cream out of Styrofoam cups using plastic spoons. Sweet relief from the summer heat!

During the week, on hot summer afternoons when I visited Mema's, Granddaddy would always offer a treat. "Won't a milkshake Scotty?" he would ask, knowing my answer was always "Yes sir!". The next question was "Vanilla or chocolate?", knowing the answer was always "Chocolate!". Granddaddy would gather the necessary ingredients. From the top freezer, homemade vanilla ice cream that was made the weekend before. From the refrigerator below, whole milk and the large mason jar of homemade chocolate syrup. The syrup was made weekly by Mema on the stove using Hershey cocoa, sugar and milk. From the cabinet above the stove, a large bottle of vanilla extract – normally used for cooking. He would scoop the ice cream into a large tea glass, cover it with chocolate syrup, fill up the glass with milk then add a dash of vanilla on top. He would mix the shake by hand, using a table fork.

Every grandchild was offered a milkshake when they visited my Mema's, and they all experienced the anticipation of watching Granddaddy make their milkshake. When the shake was completed, Granddaddy would cautiously hand the over-filled glass to you.

He told me, “Here you go, Scotty!” holding the glass with two hands.

No fast-food restaurant ever made a shake that tasted so good. The shake was not mixed completely. The ice cream was still slightly chunky with pea-sized bits and there might be a streak of chocolate on the inside of the glass. It tasted like a frozen liquid Hershey bar, but sweeter, with tiny ice crystals tickling your tongue with every swallow. It was hard to drink them slowly. When you finished drinking the shake, you used your finger to try and get that last scrape of chocolate off the inside of the glass. You always wished there had been more. I have tried to replicate this recipe for my daughters, but it’s impossible with store-bought ingredients. It’s also impossible without Granddaddy.

My grandfather passed fourteen years before my grandmother. I was in my early thirties, working at Kennedy Space Center when my father called me. “You need to get to Tallahassee now to say goodbye to Granddaddy”. I made the 4-hour drive as quickly as possible. Once at the hospital, arriving on the floor I was told, it was no mistake where my grandfather was being treated.

The sound of the family singing Baptist hymns filled the air. My grandfather’s seven children, their spouses, most of my cousins… they spilled out of the small hospital room and into the hallway. Most were standing, tears dripping from their eyes, each taking turns to have their final moments with Granddaddy. Most had been there the night and day before. Mema was sitting next to Granddaddy, holding his hand. Uncle Randy played the guitar and led us in hymns. His voice was a little louder at the beginning of each verse to keep everyone on track.

"Go speak to him Scotty, we've been here a while", Uncle Randy told me. I was tentative, edging my way through the crowded hospital room. My grandfather was propped up on the bed with his pillow from home, resting on the starched white sheets of the adjustable hospital bed. My dad was standing next to the bed, eyes bloodshot, tears running down his cheeks. I could not hold my emotions and started crying with everyone else. My grandfather weakly said, "Hey Scotty". I could barely speak. I did not know what to say. I stooped down to hug my grandfather, "Thank you for all of the milkshakes you made Granddaddy," was all I was able to get out of my mouth. There was no way for me to articulate the love and adoration that I had for him.

I couldn't bear to stay in the room for more than a few minutes after hugging Granddaddy. I had already lost my other grandfather, who had lived with us in Kentucky. He died at the age of 91. I had flashbacks of us finding him in our kitchen after his heart attack. He was found lifeless, and I held my crying Mom until the paramedics arrived.

But this was the first time I had witnessed a loved one who was physically dying in front of my eyes. We were there for many hours, different family members, the preacher, long-time friends each making their way up to the hospital bed to say their goodbyes. Prayers were said by deacons, family members and the preacher. My grandfather became too weak to speak. The nurses periodically checked his vital signs. Grandaddy's breathing became more labored and slowed.

Uncle Randy led us in the 1907 Ada Habershon hymn, "Will the Circle Be Unbroken". The word "Will" was replaced by "May". These are the words from the first verse as my family sang them.

There are loved ones in the glory,
Whose dear forms you often miss;
When you close your earthly story,
May you join them in their bliss?

May the circle be unbroken
By and by, yes, by and by?
In a better home a-waiting
In the sky, in the sky?

The Honeysuckle Heaven Gang

My parents were divorced and they both remarried in 1975. I was eleven years old. My sister, Stacey, was eight years old. Up to this point in time, we lived with my parents in Tallahassee and visited Sopchoppy on the weekends. My stepfather Russell's new business opportunity changed that arrangement. Mom and Russell bought a Ford car dealership in Berea, Kentucky. This was Russell's hometown. My mom had been there once to meet Russell's parents. Stacey and I had never been to Kentucky before.

Our parents agreed that when school was in session, that my sister and I would live in Kentucky with my mom. In the summers, we would live with my dad. So, beginning in 1976, Stacey and I spent our summers in Sopchoppy with Dad, our new stepmother Leona and two new stepsisters, Tannye and Beth. Tannye was six months older than Stacey. Beth was a year younger. Stacey and I got along better with our stepsisters than we did with each other. Two years later, Dad and Leona had a son together, they named Daniel.

After the divorce, my dad didn't have much money. He was between jobs. I remember him going door-to-door to sell his friend's latest invention. Mr. Hodge was an engineer and sometimes invented things. Dad was trying to sell Mr. Hodge's sliding glass door lock.

The lock was two 4-inch-wide thin aluminum plates hinged together. You wedged the plates between the glass and rubber seal of the door's fixed frame. To lock the door, you opened the hinged plates, blocking the door from opening. Dad's spiel started by showing the prospective customer how easy it was to break into their house through their sliding glass door, even if they had a broom handle wedged in the track. Tearing apart someone's sliding glass door didn't always go too well.

Having little money, Dad lived in the trailer that he had bought with my mom. It sat on his Sopchoppy River lot in Indian Summer. In this first summer, the single-wide trailer was going to be cramped for our 6-person family. My dad and Leona made it work, but they at once started scheming on how to improve our living arrangements.

The trailer sat four feet high on concrete blocks. It was white with bronze trim and shutters. The trailer had two entrances. The first entrance went directly into a small living room. The room had two chairs and a couch. The couch was at the end of the trailer and was directly under a window-unit air conditioner. At night, being the oldest and only boy, I was lucky enough to sleep on the couch under the air conditioner.

Separated from the living room by a counter peninsula was the small kitchen and dining area. A television sat on the counter. On the other side of the kitchen was the child's bedroom. Stacey and I used to share the room. Now all three of my sisters slept here. There was a single bunk bed and a twin bed in the room. The beds were surplus metal Army camping cots that used to belong to my Granddaddy Scott. Military mattresses with blue-striped ticking were on their wire lattice frames. They too were surplused in the 1940s. Being little over a foot apart, it was easy to jump from the top bunk to the twin bed next to it.

Down the hallway from the first bedroom was a bathroom, the second entrance and Dad and Leona's bedroom. Their bedroom also had a window unit air conditioner, and they kept their bedroom door closed. All the rooms in the trailer had built-in wood-laminated closets and cabinets, so it didn't need much furniture.

My sisters were jealous of my sleeping quarters in the trailer. The room they were in did not have an air conditioner and was brutally hot. The coolness from the living room did not quite make into their room. They depended on a small, metal, oscillating fan to circulate the air. The girls often fought if one of them changed the angle of the fan to blast it toward their bed. Stacey complained the most about the heat, because she was on the top bunk.

Dad and Leona worked every day in Tallahassee, leaving us kids to "fend for ourselves". Tallahassee was 35 miles from Sopchoppy. Leona would leave a long list of chores on the refrigerator to keep us busy. Stacey and I were not used to having lists.

"I'm not used to these hardships!" Stacey complained about the chores.

"I'm not either!" Leona agreed.

Chores alone did not occupy the long summer days for me and my sisters. At this age, we had to wait until Dad and Leona got home to swim in the river. We weren't old enough to go out on the boat. We were left at the trailer to watch TV and "play". If we had differences, we needed to resolve them ourselves. Back then, it was a long-distance call from Sopchoppy to Tallahassee. We were cautioned that the trailer "needed to be on fire" before making a call to our parents working in Tallahassee. I'm not sure why that defined the calling threshold since there was no way they could drive fast enough to put a fire out.

When a break was needed from my three sisters, I would walk from our trailer to see my cousins, Brad and David.

Their parents worked in Tallahassee also. During this time, my cousins lived on State Road 22, which was just across from my granddaddy's field. Mema and Granddaddy's house was only a mile away from the trailer in Indian Summer. Though it seemed farther when walking on a soft sand road in the heat of July. I always stopped at Mema and Granddaddy's on the way to my cousins. If only to see what type of cake was on the counter.

Usually, Brad or David would give me a ride back to the trailer. Their dad had given Brad an XR75 Honda motorcycle for his birthday in April. Later, David received a Honda Z50 minibike. When I was with my cousins, this was our primary transportation. I rode on the back of their seat with my legs held wide apart. If I held them too close, the bike's exhaust would painfully burn my calf. I still have scars.

In the afternoons, I watched TV with my sisters. Usually, we watched the *Brady Bunch* and I pretended not to like *Little House on the Prairie*. That blonde girl in it was so mean!

After Dad and Leona got home from work, we were finally able to swim in the river! Except for Leona, we all got into the river with my dad and swam to the sandbar. This is where we had the most fun.

At one end of my dad's river lot, there was a large clump of palmetto plants and honeysuckle vines hanging over the river. This is where I built a fort and later a tree house. Two tupelo trees were growing close together and one leaned out far over the river. We hammered leftover boards into the trees to create a ladder. This allowed us to climb easily into the overhanging tree and jump fifteen feet into the river below. Later, my dad added a rope swing. This area of our yard was known to all of us as "Honeysuckle Heaven".

While Leona cooked supper, we would play tag, have splash fights, or play in Honeysuckle Heaven. We challenged ourselves to jump out of the tupelo tree and make the biggest splash. We would see who could swing the highest and jump off the rope swing into the river.

After swimming and playing for almost an hour, Leona would throw a bar of soap at us, out to the sandbar. It was always Ivory soap, because Ivory was the only soap that floated. We took turns bathing with the soap, being careful not to get soap into our eyes, before getting out of the river.

Our evenings concluded with watching one of the three channels available to us, ABC, CBS or PBS. The CBS station Channel 6 and the PBS station channel 11 had a clear picture. The ABC station was fuzzy and required me to go out and turn the tall television antenna that was strapped to the side of the trailer. The NBC station in Panama City would not come in at all.

The shows we would watch included: *Happy Days*, *The Six Million Dollar Man*, *The Waltons*, and *The Sonny and Cher Show*. On Sundays we watched *Mutual of Omaha's Wild Kingdom* and *The Wonderful World of Disney*. At that time, the televisions did not have a remote control. One of us children had to get up and turn a knob to change the channel. We argued about whose turn it was to get up.

Fortunately, with so few options, we didn't have to change the channel often.

With this new arrangement to live with my dad in the summers, our parents agreed that mom and Russell would bring us down from Kentucky after the school year ended. It was my dad's responsibility to take my sister and I back to Kentucky at the end of the summer. Dad and Leona decided to incorporate our family vacations into this long road trip. The problem was, they did not own a car that all four children could fit in.

My dad still drove the 1964 1/2 Mustang and Leona drove a Volkswagen Super Beetle. When driving in Sopchoppy, the four of us children were small enough to cram into the backseat of the Mustang, which didn't have seatbelts. When we took the Volkswagen, one child had to sit in the "well", behind the back seat. These were our options, or somebody stayed at the trailer. Obviously, these travel arrangements were not safe enough for a long-distance trip to Kentucky. So, in addition to expanding our living quarters, Dad and Leona were in a difficult search for a low cost, reliable vehicle that could hold six people.

One morning, my dad drove home with hopefully the answer to their transportation prayers. He was excited. He'd found a blue, nineteen sixty-something, Ford Econoline Van. The blue was a faded metallic. On either side of the van, was a cracked and faded logo for "Zenith" in all caps.

The "Z" in Zenith was a two-foot-tall yellow lightning bolt with the bottom stroke extending under the remaining letters. Below the word zenith was a picture of a TV with multi-colored bars on the screen. The logo was superimposed over the picture of an outdoor VHF antenna like we had next to the trailer. Zenith made televisions and antennas. The van had been owned by a TV technician in the county. My dad bought it for five hundred dollars.

The van was a "cab-forward" design with a wraparound windshield. The only other windows were in the two front doors and the rear hinged barn doors. The two hinged side doors did not have windows. Cab-forward means it didn't have a hood. The van's engine was inside the cab, under a cowling between the two short bucket seats. The 3-speed manual transmission was shifted from the steering wheel stalk.

After my dad drove up, all the kids ran out from the trailer to see our new vehicle. My dad was grinning from ear to ear. He opened the side doors for us, and we jumped inside the back of the van. Behind the two front seats, the van was carpeted wall-to-wall. It was deep, thick shag-pile carpet, typical of the seventies. The carpet was burnt orange and tan colored, and it covered every square inch of the cargo space, including the doors and ceiling. There were no seats in the van except for the two up front. Once we got in, the four of us children rolled around on the carpet, like it was a new fort. We imagined ourselves playing back here all the way to Kentucky.

Well... obviously the van needed seats. My Dad had the brilliant idea of using picnic table benches. There were two perfectly good, wooden picnic benches in the front yard that were about three feet long. His thinking was that they were sturdy, cheap and immediately available. Two kids could comfortably fit on each bench. Two rows of the benches fit perfectly in the cargo space of the van! The wooden benches were cleaned up and placed on the carpet in van.

My dad was an accountant, not an engineer.

Before our long journey to Kentucky, my dad and Leona decided we should take a maiden, 35-mile trip to Tallahassee. This would evaluate the van and seating arrangements before our big trip. We were to leave at dusk to see the new Disney movie, *The Apple Dumpling Gang*.

The movie was playing in the "new" Northwood Mall theaters. I had only been to the mall a few times. The mall had space-age escalators, and the theater downstairs was right next door to Strickland's shoe store (no relation). This would be like a trip to the future! The entire family was excited about leaving Sopchoppy for an adventurous evening out.

When it was time to go, my three sisters, my cousin David and myself all loaded up in the van. We sat on the two rows of picnic benches in the back, and my dad and Leona sat in the bucket seats up front. My Dad started up the van. We were all giggling like kids going to Disney World.

As my dad let off the clutch, the van lurched forward. The sudden jerk motion caused the picnic benches to pivot backwards! All of us sitting on the benches, pivoted with them and fell on our backs with legs up in the air!

Two of my sisters were crying, my cousin and I were laughing, and my dad started cussing. My stepmother started telling Dad that the benches were a bad idea to begin with and not safe. My Dad jumped out of the van and ripped open the van's cargo door. He ordered us "Yahoos" out of the van and threw both picnic benches into the yard. He yelled at us to get back into the van and be quiet! So, we did.

"Yahoos" was the term my dad used when he was giving firm directions to all the children in the room at once. He pronounced it "Yay-Hoo". I don't ever remember it being used in a positive context. My dad had the same tone when talking about the "A-hole" drivers that cut in front of him.

After we were ten miles out of Sopchoppy, everyone felt comfortable enough to begin talking again. My sisters started singing their songs. The walls and floor of van vibrated. The engine under its plastic cowling roared so loud that we had to yell to be heard.

Sitting on the floor in the back of the van, we kids could see nothing but each other and wall-to-wall shag carpet. There were no indicators from that vantage point, telling us how close we were to Tallahassee. We just felt the vibration and the swaying back and forth as dad drove the winding curves of Highway 319.

From the very start of the ride, there was a faint smell of something burning. The rusty exhaust system was leaking fumes, and they permeated through the van's floorboard.

The fumes were only lightly filtered through the shag carpet on the floor. After about 15 miles, the van's interior started to get smoky, and the smell became worse. The shag carpet became saturated with the van's exhaust.

My sisters were coughing. I got on my knees to open the backdoor tilt windows for ventilation. Through the windows, I could see a billowing, bluish-gray cloud. Cars were in a line behind us. They were flashing their lights and honking their horns, trying to pass us.

"Dad, there are a lot of cars behind us flashing their lights!" I dutifully informed my dad.

"I know son!" my dad yelled back.

My sisters got on their knees to see behind us. My stepmother had a familiar concerned look, and my dad became more agitated. Looking through the back windows, we watched as drivers risked their life to escape our cloud of smoke. Their only hope of doing so was to pass us on the curvy two-lane highway.

Sometimes they would almost escape the cloud, only to duck back in after seeing a fast-approaching car. We knew they saw a car because we heard its horn blare as it passed us from the front. One by one, the cars in the exhaust cloud escaped to pass us. My dad labeling each car's driver as they sped by: "Maniac!", "Stupid idiot!", "Did you see that guy!?"

Somehow, the van made it to Tallahassee. When we stopped at the first traffic light in Tallahassee, the smoke caught us and engulfed the van. This made everyone cough and gag, including Dad and Leona. My sisters now complained louder. When the light turned green, my dad popped the clutch, and a loud explosion came from under the van! We all squealed!

When we arrived at Northwood Mall, dad dropped us off at the back of the parking lot. Dad stayed in the van, keeping the motor running. His next mission was to look for STP oil treatment. We "yahoos" and my stepmother went in to see the movie.

In the mall, we rode down the escalator. We marveled at the storefronts on the way to the theater. *The Apple Dumpling Gang* movie was an awesome movie. It told the story of three orphans traveling with the gambler, Mr. Donovan, in the wild west. The movie starred actors we were familiar with on TV: Bill Bixby, Tim Conway and Don Knotts. The movie's wagon trip in the wild west made us excited for our Kentucky road trip to come. We quoted the movie all the way home.

We ended up not taking the Zenith Van to Kentucky. In fact, the Apple Dumpling journey was our only family trip in the vehicle. My dad never drove the van out of Sopchoppy again. He eventually sold the van.

Next, Dad's car search led him to a used Ford Grand Torino station wagon. The large Torino was metallic forest-green with fake wood paneling on the sides. It looked just like the car you saw in the Griswold *Vacation* movie. It even had seats. A split bench seat in the front, a bench seat in the middle and a jump seat that folded into the cargo space. This was to be our mode of transportation to Kentucky for years to come.

Before our next summer, my dad moved the trailer to my granddaddy's land across the road. He put it behind the Honey House. This gave my dad room to later build a house on his river property. Since the trailer was cramped when my sister and I visited, my stepmother convinced my dad to add a second smaller trailer. It needed to be done before next summer, when Stacey and I arrived.

Dad found a one bedroom, single-wide trailer that was cream colored with green trim. The shorter "new-to-us" trailer was parked parallel, four feet from our old trailer. With great ingenuity and my uncle's help, dad connected the two trailers. Between two exterior doors, they built a hallway out of two-by-fours, plywood, and tar paper. The hallway was on concrete blocks at the same floor-level as the two trailers. Dad named our new household after my stepmother, Leona. He called it "Leona's Rig".

We were in the "Rig" for one or two summers while my dad built his dream home on the river. My sleeping quarters moved from the couch into the room that my sisters used to share. My sisters moved in the "new" trailer, on the other side of the hallway my dad built. This gave me a new appreciation for air conditioning. I got to keep the oscillating fan in my room. It always pointed at my bed.

Other than the added square footage, the biggest improvement my dad made was a motorized TV antenna. No longer did I have to go outside and rotate the antenna pole when we wanted to watch ABC. He had a book-sized box with a large dial on top of the TV. The dial could be rotated to a heading that corresponded with North, South, East and West. A turn of the dial would cause the motor outside to rotate the antenna in that direction. It was a modern miracle!

I've often wondered if my dad bought this miracle device from the same guy that sold him the Ford van. The antenna motor was the better deal!

In the few years that followed, my dad's career with the State of Florida progressed to the point where he could afford to build a house. With us living in Leona's Rig, my dad, Granddaddy and Uncle Bernie dug the foundation. The house was built in the same exact location that the trailer once stood, at the highest point on my dad's river lot in Indian Summer. Leona and my dad had designed the house so that each of the children could have their own room. Mine was in the basement.

After the house was built, it wasn't long before my dad and Leona had a child of their own. My dad only agreed to have a child if Leona guaranteed it would be a boy. Somehow, she was able to satisfy this promise. They named my little brother Daniel, after my dad's older brother.

A baby in the house, ten years younger than their closest sibling, changes the family dynamic. For us, the biggest change was making two of my sisters share a room again.

Thankfully we still had the Grand Torino station wagon. Daniel was able to sit in his car seat between dad and Leona in the front bench seat. I was pushed into the jump seat with Beth, it was located in the cargo area. The station wagon allowed us to still travel all together.

Between the ages of thirteen to sixteen, I worked in my dad's feed store This was my dad's on-again, off-again entrepreneurial diversion, the Sopchoppy Feed & Seed. Since he wasn't making any money with the store, he called it a community service. In the store there was feed, seed, fertilizer, and hardware.

In the summers, I had to work in the Feed Store for a dollar an hour. My Dad told me this was a great opportunity because he wasn't taking out any taxes. I didn't know any better. By my third year, I was making two dollars an hour which was close to the Florida minimum wage of $3.10. Still a good deal I was told.

The Feed Store building was old, it was small, and it was hot. It had unpainted wood floors, a tin roof and no air conditioning. You could sweep the floor a dozen times and never get the fine dust out from between the boards. Sopchoppy Florida summers were very hot. The main store had a tall ceiling. The storage room ceiling was only 6 or 7 feet, sloping down. The hot tin roof was right above your head, and the only ventilation came from the open back door. This made the storage room 10-15 degrees hotter than the main store.

The only source of cold air in the entire store was a 1950's era Coke machine with 8-ounce glass bottles inside its door. On days that I had to unload the feed truck; I was drenched with sweat. Relief came from a bottle of Grape Nehi and putting my face inside the door of the Coke machine.

The main store had a wide assortment of seed, nails, hardware, livestock medicine and other sundries. During the first years, my dad stocked Red Wing boots in the store. Trying to guess the style, size, and color boots preferred by customers in a town with a population of only 450 was probably not the best business plan. Those that wanted boots in Sopchoppy already had them. Those that didn't have boots yet shopped for them in Tallahassee.

One unique item carried in the Feed Store was the "Catfish Hunter Throwing Arm and Wrist Trainer". Another Mr. Hodge invention in which I think my dad had an investment. It was two leather straps; one went around your bicep and the other on your forearm. A brass double-ended swivel snap hook attached to the two straps, keeping your elbow bent at 90 degrees. It included a book by Major League Baseball Pitcher Catfish Hunter "How to improve your throwing in 3-6 weeks!". We never sold one in Sopchoppy.

Often, hours would go by without a customer. Boredom was a major issue. We had no cell phones. There was no TV. The AM radio would only pick up one or two stations. After multiple laps walking the store, I would stop and take a big whiff of the horse feed. The highlight of the day was if my cousin David stopped by. He was always entertaining.

We would joke about the town's colorful residents, plot our evening activities or plan a weekend camping trip.

Occasionally, Mr. Ronald would come over from the Dixie Dandy. Ronald Langston's store adjoined the Feed Store by way of the stockroom. Mr. Ronald would always be wearing his white, full-length apron and a big smile. He was co-owner of the Feed Store with my dad. After briefly asking how I was doing, he'd tell me about his son Steven going to school at Auburn for the next ten minutes. This was repeated two to three times a week.

I drove the 1964 Mustang to open the Feed Store at 9 AM every morning and parked it across the street next to the loafer's bench store. I drove it in the summers, before I had a driver's license, sitting on a red square throw pillow so I could see over the steering wheel. After getting my license, my dad gave me the Mustang for my 16th birthday, and we took it to Kentucky. I also drove the Super Beetle when I was in Sopchoppy for the summer.

Every day after he came home from work, my dad would stop by the feed store on his way home. He looked inside the cash register, looked at the receipts for the day and told me he would see me at home soon. I would close the store at Six PM. I got Saturday's off when my dad worked in the store.

While I worked at the Feed Store, my sisters helped Leona take care of Daniel and perform their normal chores. After Leona went back to work, Daniel as a toddler was taken to the Happy Times Nursery School in Crawfordville. One day, Daniel changed the family dynamics even more.

My sisters got the call at home while I was at the Feed Store; our parents wouldn't be home until very late. Daniel had a run-in with a tree at Happy Times. He had broken his leg. Daniel was sent home in a cast. The cast went from his knee, up his thigh and around his waist to the other leg. There was a stick between the cast on both legs, preventing Daniel from moving.

After a few days of pain, Daniel was back to himself except he couldn't sit or walk. It took two of us to lift him and move him from his bed to the couch. We all signed the white cast, which covered one-third of his body. I drew a Woody Woodpecker and a pointing arrow on the inside of his thigh. Daniel wore a pair of dad's boxer shorts to cover up holes in the cast that were necessary for bodily functions.

My dad partially solved Daniel's mobility problem. He went by Sears on his way home and bought a wooden Creepy-Crawly. This was designed for a car mechanic to slide on their back to work under a car. It had omni-directional wheels and a small head pillow at one end.

Daniel loved it! Lying on his stomach on the Creepy-Crawly, he could move around the house again. Using his arms in a swimming motion, he propelled himself on the pine floors. My sisters fed him from the dining room table, like he was a dog. Dad was pleased with his ingenuity. Leona worried about her new floors and Daniel's self-esteem.

Over the next five weeks, relatives and friends who came to visit were a little shocked to see Daniel in his current condition. My red-headed little brother with his lower body in a cast was rolling around the floor on his stomach, wearing boxer shorts that were too big. He was rolling under the dining table and around the couches. The rest of his siblings were watching TV, now jaded to his movements. Daniel held his head up like he was swimming and trying to hold it above water. He had a huge grin on his face!

"Sometimes Happy Times aren't always that happy." That was how my dad explained Daniel's situation.

The Fourth of July

Before Sopchoppy became known for having a Worm Grunting Festival -yes, a worm festival - it was known for having the best Fourth of July celebration in Wakulla County. Heck, the best in north Florida! My first memory of this festivity was in 1976. This being our country's 200th birthday, people were extremely proud. Every advertisement capitalized on the bicentennial. People flew their American Flags all year. Red, white, and blue colors were everywhere. With so many people in attendance and this ground swell in patriotism, 1976 had a significant impact on future celebrations.

At this time, the town held the celebration at the Sopchoppy High School, next to the new gymnasium. The high school is now a historic site and is in the U. S. National Register of Historic Places. Sopchoppy citizens funded construction of the school, originally built in 1924 in a Spanish style using limestone rocks. Future additions in the 1930's were constructed similarly. The "Spanish Mission" looking limestone gymnasium across the street was then in need of significant repair.

When someone left the doors open on the old gym, my cousins and I would skateboard on the basketball court, creating ramps to jump over the holes in the floor. Constructed of thick heavy stones with large broken windows at the top, the temperature in the old gym was cooler than being outside. The new gymnasium was rectangular, built out of concrete and looked typical of 1970's modern construction.

1976 was Sopchoppy's 3rd annual celebration and would be its biggest so far. The town billed it as "Wakulla County Pays Tribute to America". The thirty-page program for the celebration expressed, "The goal of the Bicentennial is to forge a new national commitment, a new spirit of '76, a spirit which vitalizes the ideals for which the revolution was fought; a spirit which will unite the Nation in purpose and in dedication to the advancement of human welfare as it moves into its Third century."

These were lofty goals for a town of 450 people, but the goals were held by all during this patriotic time. Of the thirty pages in the program, all except three were business advertisements and messages from individuals across Wakulla County. The local restaurants, grocery stores, realtors, banks, gas stations... they all wanted to be associated with this historic event held in tiny little Sopchoppy.

Starting at 11:00 A.M., Sopchoppy First Baptist Church's own Reverend Glenn Lawhon gave the invocation to begin the event. The Wakulla Veterans of Foreign Wars raised the flag in ceremony. Congressman Don Fuqua gave his Independence Day address. The Wakulla High School Band played the national anthem and the parade through Sopchoppy began!

Sopchoppy parades are different than what you see before the Tournament of Roses Bowl or at the Macy's Thanksgiving Parade. The Sopchoppy "floats" are constructed by community members on farm trailers using chicken wire and crepe paper stuffing. The local churches each have a float. Ladies from the church would sit in rocking chairs that sat on a farm trailer. Holding their Bibles, they waved at the audience as they rode by, rocking away.

"Sopchoppy's Finest" lone volunteer fire truck drives through with children on top. Local county and city politicians ride in convertibles, sometimes sitting on top of the back seat, and throw candy to the children in the audience. You always get way more candy during the election years.

The parade starts at the beginning of Rose Street, right off Highway 319, and it continues all the way to Faith

Avenue. People line both sides of the street, trying to cool themselves with the paper hand fans passed out by promoting politicians. Children dash in front of oncoming parade participants, to grab the candy that did not make it as far as the sidewalk.

Anyone with a decorated tractor, lawn mower or bike was welcome to be in the parade. My cousin David and I were in the parade for years. Sometimes decorating our banana seat bikes with crepe paper and playing cards dragging against the wheel spokes. Once we walked our "invisible dogs" that were souvenirs from the Six Flags Over Georgia Amusement Park. The "dogs" were a wire-stiffened rope with an expanded dog harness at the end. We shook the leashes at the crowd, walking the pretend dogs. David and I barked and growled to add realism. The crowd was amazed!

Over a dozen police and State Trooper cars were at the beginning and end of the parade, sirens blasting. Crawfordville's fire trucks would come. The local forestry service pulled their dirt movers chained on top of a trailer. Dried mud still clinging to the bulldozer's tank-like tracks. Mike's Marine Supply pulled a decorated fishing boat. The Shiners wearing their Fez hats and vests rode Honda Goldwing motorcycles in formation. Their stunts include frantically doing figure-eights in the street, passing only inches from the crowd. The crowd was thrilled! but also fearing for their safety.

At the end of the parade, the Wakulla County sheriff and his deputies rode tall on their horses. They slowly walked down the street with the sheriff in front and the Deputies in formation behind him like a flock of birds. They wore their Kelly-green uniforms, gold black-tipped star badges and white straw cowboy hats. Behind them, followed two Wakulla prison inmates, on work release. They were wearing orange coveralls with wide black stripes.

The convicts pushed a wheelbarrow and carried flat ended shovels. Their purpose was to collect the horse manure left by the deputies' horses. When a horse pooped the parade audience cheered! Then they giggled as the inmates performed their clean-up duty. The two prisoners took turns shoveling the manure. The horses' actions and the inmates' reactions were replayed along the entire parade route.

This became a Sopchoppy Parade tradition. During the first years, the prisoner clean-up crew looked a little humiliated, but sometimes it looked like they were just glad to be in the sun and enjoying the people. There was always an armed deputy walking behind the inmates to remind them not to have too much fun.

After the parade, all migrated to where the festival was to take place, and the Sopchoppy High School was well within walking distance. In 1976, the Florida State University Circus gave three performances. A stage was set up behind the school, and a series of gospel groups and country bands entertained the crowd until dark. The headliner this year was Grand Ole Opry Star Hank Locklin, best known for his 1960 hit "Please Help Me, I'm Falling". Bobby Rice, "from Nashville, Tennessee" also played. In the middle of the afternoon, Sopchoppy's own rock band "The Wakulla" played Allman Brothers and Lynyrd Skynyrd hits. The local band has always been a favorite for the festival.

Adding to the entertainment in 1976 were the Swamphollow Skydivers and square dancing by the Tallahassee Crosstrailers. A raffle was held and two first prizes were given. In the first drawing a four horsepower Evinrude outboard was given away. The second drawing was for a 12-gauge shotgun, donated by the Olin Corporation from St Marks. Olin made gunpowder there, so the raffle donation was appropriate

The Lions Club sold hamburgers, raising money for their cause. Churches sold baked goods. Local beekeepers sold honey. People brought their arts and crafts to sell. Once, I even set up a booth to sell my own artwork. I think I sold a painting for five dollars!

All these festivities served as a build-up to what everyone came to see, the Sopchoppy fireworks! This was always the biggest display of an imported gunpowder light show in the area, rivaling Tallahassee. The show would start with a series of spinning sparklers at ground level, positioned just 150 feet from the music stage. This gave warning to the crowd, who nervously stepped back several yards, remembering the fireworks were ignited by Sopchoppy volunteers, not professionals.

Then a series of launches would be heard, Thump! Thump! Thump! The crowd eagerly expected the explosion of colorful expanding light cascades high in the air. A chorus of Oohs! and Awes! were heard in appreciation of the display. Intermittently a mortar would launch instead, providing a thunderous boom instead of the beloved light show. The crowd screamed and belatedly covered their ears.

In 1976, twenty minutes into the fireworks display, the oohs and awes were replaced by murmurs throughout the crowd. "What is this falling from the sky?" asked two or three people.

Shadows of charred paper and ash had begun to fall into the audience. Smelling something burning, women were asking if their hair was on fire. Flammable hair spray kept their Bea Arthur Maude hairstyles in place; this put them at great risk.

Within five minutes, someone noticed that embers were falling on top of the brand-new gymnasium. The embers still glowed with the potential to cause great harm. Sopchoppy's Finest mobilized, the volunteer firetruck was staged and ready. They doused the gym roof with water and the crowd retreated farther. The fireworks display continued as "The Stars and Stripes Forever" played over the loudspeakers. The crowd laughed and cheered at the water and firework combination on display.

The 1976 fireworks display would become the impetus for Sopchoppy to build a City Park on the Sopchoppy River, away from the town's historical buildings. The park was named Myron B. Hodge, also known as the "Worm King" of Sopchoppy. He owned a store that sold fish bait to over 100 retailers. Earth worms were the trade item that

Sopchoppy would later become known for. The park was 35 acres and founded on Park Avenue. An elevated concrete stage was built that included two bathrooms on the backside. Sopchoppy could now safely expand its July celebration without fear of burning down the town.

In the years that followed, Sopchoppy's Fourth of July Celebration became a fixture for the surrounding area. The city organizers took pride in the musical acts they were able to book for this small-town event. One year getting Tom Wopat, Luke Duke from the legendary TV show *The Dukes of Hazard*. Who knew he could sing? The town parade's size and attraction stayed the same even after the patriotic draw of the bicentennial. Always being slightly bigger during an election year.

With the new park, instead of walking to the high school after the parade, people now drove in a line to the new venue, down the dusty unpaved Park Avenue. In the dry season, dust was kicked up by the parade of cars so badly that you couldn't see ten feet in front of you. My dad couldn't stand the idea of getting in this "mess" of a crowd and parking amongst them.

From my dad's aggravation with the parking situation our tradition of travelling by boat to the Fourth of July Celebration was born. It was possible since the park was on banks of the Sopchoppy River. It took a half hour to trek by boat from my dad's house in Indian Summer to Myron B. Hodge Park. The river winds and turns and fallen trees create an everchanging mine field of stumps in the water.

We made this first journey in my Granddaddy Scott's old fiberglass V-Hull boat. There were two built-in bench seats and a small triangular platform on the bow. My dad attached the Evinrude, hooked up the red metal gas tank and we loaded the boat with orange canvas life jackets. My dad sat on the only boat cushion.

The trip to the park was exhilarating, my dad expertly navigated the boat on plane around the twists of the river. He knew where every stump lurked beneath the water. We would occasionally see a small alligator and my dad would veer the boat into its path, in efforts to persuade the gator to go elsewhere. I sat on the bow, wind blowing in my hair. My stepsisters sat with Leona on top of the middle seat and Stacey sat with my dad in the back. We all wore our bathing suits.

After a little less than thirty minutes, we were at the park. There was no dust. Parking was as simple as tying our bow line to an overhanging branch. We were right behind the Lion's Club hamburger pavilion. Only two other boats were there.

We did it! My dad smiled, proud that he had beat the system. He had brought his family to the celebration. We had a delightful boat ride getting there. We avoided the dust and suffering associated with parking. My dad had a full cooler of adult beverages, which weren't allowed in the park. Life was good!

The children were set free. We found our cousins and family who had staked claims with blankets in front of the bandstand. We saw Granddaddy cooking hamburgers and our dad let us buy one for lunch. After perusing around all the temporary shade structures with wares for sale, we made our way back to the boat. We swam in the river with a dozen other children, trying to find the sandbar to stand on. The chill of the river water offered a welcome reprieve from the summer heat.

Somehow, my dad found the patience to stay until the fireworks started. It might have been because he could enjoy adult beverages in the boat. We again saw the tradition of water city manager, Bill Stevens setting the ground sparklers ablaze. Spinning sparks simultaneously flew into the air and on to the ground, delighting the audience. The aerial fireworks were now fired over the river. Ashes fell into the woods instead of on spectators.

We returned to the boat tied up at the bank for the finale. This vantage point offered the perfect balance of safety and allowed us to see the reflection of fire fountains in the water. We applauded with the crowd when the light show was complete. It was a successful celebration!

It was now pitch dark. The Moon had not risen. The fireworks no longer lit up the banks of the river. It was time to go. My dad handed me the silver metal Sears Explorer flashlight holding two rusty Ray-O-Vac D-size batteries inside. Was this to light our way back? He cranked the motor. It smoked to life. After putting it in gear to head upriver, we were now on our way home.

We were on a black river, with black mud banks under a black sky. I pointlessly waved the dim flashlight back and forth searching for black stumps hidden under the water's surface. Going slow since he couldn't see, Dad couldn't put the boat on plane as he did on our trip to the park. The boat was now floating six inches deeper in the water. The tide was lower, so the river was narrower, and some logs were even sticking up above the surface of the water.

"Hold the damn light still!" my dad yelled.

This was soon after the motor clipped one of many underwater threats. After striking the third stump, he told Leona to pass him the flashlight. I handed it to her and my dad grabbed it. He held the silver flashlight above his head, clinching it with his right fist, as he guided the boat tiller with his left hand. Attempting to shine the light over Leona and my sister's heads, he told us to get our heads down. I was now left on the bow, crouching so the light could go over me, still trying to discern stumps from reflections barely visible under the pitch-dark sky.

"Something's biting me!" cried one of my sisters in the boat.

"Me too!" cried another.

Mosquitoes previously deterred by daylight and the artificial wind of a fast-moving boat, now descended on us with the cover of darkness. They ravenously attacked our bare skin. The high-pitched whine of their wings dive-bombed our ears.

"Where's the can of Off!" yelled Leona, fumbling with empty cans and coolers at the bottom of boat. The sloped V-hull pushed our stuff into a pile in the middle of the boat.

She, and all of us, were now looking for the orange spray can of petroleum repellent that might offer us a little protection. It was under these beverage cans somewhere...

We hit another stump, a big one. The boat heaved over the fallen log like a car with no suspension over an unseen speed hump. The motor's propellor came fully out of the water with a loud rush. After lurching back, then forward again with regained propulsion, the motors lower unit settled back into the black water.

"Boy!! are you watching out up there!", my dad yelled.

"Yes dad!" I answered as I returned to my post at the bow.

After over an hour of mosquito bites, banging stumps and cussing from my dad, we rounded a dark river bend and saw the beacon of our trailer's porch light. We all sighed looking forward to liberation from the heat, mosquitoes, the boat and the family comradery.

After that, our river trips to the city park for the Fourth of July were truncated to ensure we returned well before dark. My sisters and I missed seeing the fireworks at the park. We missed the crowd's oohs and awes after seeing the multi-color fountain of sparks fall. We missed the screams after the loud explosions of surprise mortars.

Dad and Leona promised us something better than the park's fireworks! We were going to have our own fireworks show at home, at the trailer. Once darkness fell, we all went outside. Leona opened a small, narrow cardboard box and let each of us pull out a skinny, silver coated wire. We looked at them curious as to how this was going to be fun.

Our reward was getting the opportunity to run around the yard with Sparklers. Sparklers are children-unfriendly metal sticks coated with fuel and oxidizers. The metal powder coating emits giant bright white sparks when they burn at 2,000 degrees Fahrenheit. Dad lit each of our sticks with his Bic lighter. We ran around the yard with fire sticks! We painted our names in the darkness. The intense light leaving light trails for all to briefly see.

"This is more fun than staying at the Park." my dad assured us.

Half of the sparklers were always saved in the box so we could enjoy them on another "special occasion". Our fireworks fun was fleeting. Inevitably one of my sisters (usually Stacey) would grab the wrong end of the sparkler after it burnt out. She screamed with intense pain, dropped the scalding wire, running in circles and shaking her hand violently in the air. Her actions were a useless attempt to escape from the agony.

Leona would try to console my sister. She took the casualty to the bathroom. and treated the second-degree burn with Neosporin and a Band-Aid. The rest of us tried to convince dad to let us have another sparkler.

"We're done!" he yelled, signaling that fun-time was over.

After being sent to bed, we spent the rest of the night in our bunks. Unable to sleep with the burn victim whimpering all night. All of us now regretting her brief lapse in judgment.

A few years after 1976, my cousin David and I got bored with being in the parade. We were too cool to dart into the road and snatch up candy. Thankfully, the Sopchoppy Fourth of July Committee decided to add a canoeing race to the festivities. The canoe race started way up in Mount Beasor at Oak Park Cemetery Bridge and finished at Myron Hodge City Park. This is a 10-mile canoe trip on the Sopchoppy River.

Mount Beasor isn't a mountain. It's a little community with a church that is found on Smith Creek Highway. It's a couple of miles past Indian Summer. After leaving the highway, you follow a rarely grated washboard dirt road. Stay left at the fork, continuing to Steven C. Revell Road. A short concrete bridge is in the middle of the woods on a fire road primarily used by locals and hunters. Dad and Bobby Jack used to drive us through here when hunting.

David had access to a Mohawk fiberglass canoe. On the mornings of the race, which coincides with the Fourth of July Celebration, my dad would haul us to the launch point. Sometimes he would borrow Granddaddy's truck.

Our preparations for the race consisted of the following: David and I lifted the canoe into the bed of the truck. We threw an orange canvas life jacket and boat cushion into the boat, because my dad reminded us. All but once we remembered the paddles. David and I rode in the back of the truck to keep the canoe from flying out on the bumpy roads. The canoe bounced violently as my dad aggressively drove us on the fire road. Once at the bridge, David and I unloaded the canoe and our gear.

"Have fun." my dad told us, never getting out of the truck, and he left us.

We carried the canoe to the edge of the steep riverbank. Carefully, I would climb down the mud trail crisscrossed with exposed tree roots. David eased the canoe down the bank behind me. I trusted that David would hold the bow line as the canoe was lowered. Sometimes that trust was broken.

When this happened, I bolted down the bank like Indiana Jones trying to outrun a boulder. The canoe followed me, bouncing off tree roots as it bounded down the steep bank. To escape death, I jumped into the water from midway up the bank. The canoe stopped before following me into the water because it hung up on an exposed tree root. David stood at the top of the bank laughing at the stunt I performed trying to escape a collision.

Once the canoe was safely in the water with us inside, we checked the fiberglass hull for leaks. We had a large, rusty coffee can a.k.a. "worm bucket" in case water was seeping. We paddled slowly behind the starting line, which was on the other side of concrete bridge's pilings.

In the water around us were mostly paddlers from Tallahassee. All were adults. Some looked like they paddled canoes for leisurely recreation, wearing white pants and bright polo shirts. Three of the paddlers were hard core racers.

The racers were in 18-foot long, sleek, wood-laminated kayaks. They sat with their butts on the floor of the boat with a spray skirt around their chest. They were wearing life preservers like we would see on professional stuntman at Cypress Gardens. Their flimsy striped caps were like the Italian bike racers in the movie *Breaking Away*. The twin blades of their single paddle had funky curves in them, and their paddle was leashed to the boat.

David and I were modestly dressed - shirtless in our Sundek rainbow board shorts and wearing cheap K-mart flip flops. I sat high on the Mohawk canoe's bow seat, perched on my dad's boat cushion. I had a 3 ½-foot long wooden paddle with an Indian head logo on the blade. David sat at the stern on our only orange life vest. His wooden paddle was as tall as he was. He held on to its shaft; the intended paddle grip was a foot above his hands. We considered ourselves proud veteran paddlers, but we only used the canoe occasionally to fish and explore, never in a long race.

We all waited until someone leaned over the bridge railing and said it was close enough to 11-AM.

"Get Ready, Get Set, Go!" they finally yelled down.

The three dudes in the fancy kayaks wearing their hats backwards took off! Behind them, the recreational paddlers wearing polo shirts started to move. Four of them were in tandem canoes, a little longer than ours. David and I followed, digging our wooden paddles from Sears deep into the black water.

The Sopchoppy river around the Oak Park bridge was very different than at our trailer. It is narrow, only ten-foot wide, with canyon-like riverbanks. The bluffs on either side of the river are over thirty feet high and heavily wooded. Lining the river are limestone rock walls and old cypress trees. The water only runs downstream, unaffected by the tides. River levels and water speed fluctuate greatly based on the amount of recent rainfall. This can make the canoe trip a leisurely paddle or turn it into a river trip with Class III rapids.

Luckily, leading up to this canoe race, the weather was dry. It was also 95-degrees with 90-percent humidity. David and I started the race very strong. We navigated the narrow river twists like a Mississippi river barge, racing past a curve then aggressively paddling in opposite directions to correct our heading. We passed the first pair of recreational canoeists before going under our first landmark, the Mount Beasor Bridge. We were feeling good about our chances!

Mount Beasor bridge is on wood pilings that are close to the tall banks of the river; you must choose the correct gap between them to avoid any debris caught up. After this point, the river widens, and the surrounding terrain flattens out. The straight-aways get longer and the river curve angles become more obtuse. The water speed decelerates. Instead of cypress knots and sandbars being the obstacle, tupelo trees and live oaks hang over the water's edge. If you get too close, you might get a face full of a banana spider's web.

A banana spider can have leg spans reaching five inches. Their webs are huge, sometimes spanning branches over six feet apart. The brown and yellow spider sits in the middle of the web, awaiting its prey. They look like a hairless Tarantula. Being in the front seat of the canoe, I was intensely aware of this river hazard.

As the river's flow slowed, so did we. I could feel my arms starting to cramp up. The hectic pace that I started paddling with became steadily more deliberate. Occasionally, I would glance back at David.

"Hey! How come you're not paddling!" I challenged him.

"Scotty, I'm steering the boat!" was David's reply.

He was using the long paddle like a steering oar from Tom Sawyer's raft.

"You need to paddle too!" was my plea.

To emphasize this point I rested my paddle across both sides of the canoe. My break did not last long. I was forced to resume paddling after my head was wrapped by a banana spider's web. I frantically brushed the sticky silk strand from my head and shoulders, looking all over my body for the giant spider that spun it. Fortunately, there was no sign of the Orbweaver. I resumed paddling.

Now the river was even wider. Instead of going around the bend like a river barge, we attacked the curves like a race car driver – hoping to minimize any necessary effort. When necessary, I ducked under low-hanging branches keeping a watchful eye for spiders. We were approaching Tupelo Island, the next big landmark and our theoretical mid-point of the race.

"Scotty, I got to pee!" David complained.

Tupelo Island was a welcome port of call. We easily grounded the canoe on its wide sand bank and stepped out of the boat. After stretching our arms into the air to relax our muscles, we walked to the edge of the woods to relieve our bladders. It was David's call to pause our race, but I needed a break as well. With our backs to the river, we almost didn't notice the man and woman in the tandem canoe passing by the large sandbar. We quickly fastened the Velcro of our board shorts and nonchalantly turned, resuming our stretches.

Our stop gave us enough new-found energy to retake our position, but not much else. Our paddling cadence declined once again. A large blister was forming between my thumb and index finger. I tried to adjust my paddle grip to avoid the pain.

Before long, we were in the familiar waters of Indian Summer. In the wider river, the trees no longer gave us shade from the sun. I could feel my back and shoulders getting hot. We started seeing familiar structures. When we saw the A-frame house, we knew we were on the straightaway going in front of my dad's house.

As we approached my dad's, we could make out the pale skin of my family's torsos sticking out of the black water. They were standing on the sandbar in front of my dad's house. They started screaming and cheering when they saw us. David and I naturally picked up our pace to make a good impression.

Tannye and Stacey were at the end of the sandbar closest to us. I could see that they had bad intentions. David and I instinctively paddled the boat to deeper water, closer to my dad's house. Their plan was to tip us over, they said as payback for some perceived meanness we had done. We now stroked the water furiously, propelling the canoe and us out of harm's way.

Defeated, my sisters resorted to splashing us with water. The water felt good on my red-hot back. David used his paddle to return fire, putting twice as much water into their faces. Gulping and gasping for air, they retreated to the sandbar.

At the end of the sandbar stood my dad in waist deep water. He was holding something.

"Here, you might need this!" my dad said as he motioned us towards him.

He handed us my green-insulated, stainless-steel boy scout canteen, full of water. I reached out to grab it as David used his paddle like a rudder.

"Thanks dad!" I said, grateful for the needed nourishment.

My dad told us how many canoeists were in front of us. We were only three bends behind our nearest competitors. Immediately, the next bend took us out of sight from my family. In less than 10 bends, we would be inside Sopchoppy city limits. I screwed off the chain-linked top of the canteen and gulped swallows of the cool water my dad provided. Before halfway emptying it, I passed the open canteen back to David.

After passing the Sopchoppy swimming hole, which is across the street from the Methodist and Baptist churches, we approached Bully's dock on the river. The river's tide had begun to turn. The water was now rising, and we were paddling in the opposite direction of the current. We passed two more canoeists on this straightaway. Ahead of us, we heard screaming. There were unmistakable sounds of children laughing and adult men yelling back at them with authority.

After rounding the bend after Bully's, we saw what the commotion was about. My younger cousins and their friends were standing on the bridge crossing Stage Road 22. They were heckling the canoe racers passing underneath and were armed with water balloons. David and I knew that we were their prime targets. We picked up the pace.

My cousins aligned themselves on the section of bridge they thought we might pass under. David and I quickly scouted the bridge pilings for any caught-up logs that might hinder our route. We opted to go between the pilings closest to the bridge's concrete embankment. I ignored the blister on my hand where the skin had completely peeled off. We swiftly made our way under the bridge, only glancing to see four shirtless boys wielding brightly colored water balloons. One held a ballon in each hand. The others held a ballon raised in one hand, cradling more in their arms. We put our heads down for what was to come.

Fortunately, our cousins had poor aim. The balloons hit the sides and bottom of our canoe, but we took no direct hits to our heads. When they hit the boat, balloons exploded into splashes of water. We withstood the firepower of over a dozen balloons. There was over a half inch of water at the bottom of the canoe. As we passed under the bridge, our cousins raced to the other side to get in their final blows.

Luckily, they ran out of ammunition. David let loose his maniacal laugh as I bailed out water with the worm bucket.

Only five bends and six long straight sections of river left to go. The water current was now strongly pushing back on our advancement. The adrenalin we experienced from the water balloon attack was gone. Our canteen was empty, and it joined our worm bucket on the bottom of the hull. Our backs were burning.

"Scotty, your back is red!" David said reminding me of my suffering.

The last bend before the City Park has a short straightaway. We could hear the music coming from the grandstand. As we get closer, we can smell hamburgers cooking on the bank. Finally, we could see children swimming in the river next to the park.

"Here comes another one!", a child alerts everyone within earshot.

David and I give it one final push, showing off in front of the few people near the water. Our muscles were at their breaking point. Sweat drenched our hair, and it poured from our bodies. I was starting to smell David from across the boat and I'm sure he could smell me.

We didn't care about our appearance, our smell or anything else. We made our last final push, and we coasted the canoe into the bank right below the Lions club pavilion. We did it!

Our bodies collapsed, dropping the paddles that had been clutched almost four hours. With our hands gripping the canoe gunwales, we deliberately leaned far enough to overturn the canoe into the water. The paddles floated and I hastily grabbed for my canteen and worm bucket before they sank. We soaked in the water for 10-15 minutes. This was the least pain in my hand for hours. Pulling the canoe to the bank to right it, we put our few belongings into the hull. Both of us sat on the bank hearing the people behind us enjoying the celebration.

We came in first place for a tandem canoe in our age group. I'm pretty sure we were the only ones in our age group. It didn't matter. We had overcome banana spiders, sisters, cousins, water balloons and heatstroke. There could be no bigger sense of accomplishment. It would take days for us to recover.

Sopchoppy never held their celebration on Sunday if it coincided with the Fourth of July. The city council members knew their constituents would never stand for it. Some of the council members were also church deacons, so celebrating the holiday publicly on Sunday was never going to happen.

After a celebration was held the day before Sunday, there would be a weary congregation at the Baptist church the next day. You could smell the Solarcaine emanating from sunburns on people's necks, faces and bald heads. Some in the congregation were pre-occupied with their wounds like 2nd degree sparkler burns, blistered hands, sunburns or too many boat drinks. Still dehydrated and tired, it would take a lot to inspire the people that dragged themselves into church that day.

Sopchoppy Baptist church had a remedy that could wake this crowd up. It was my Uncle Randy. He took it upon himself to be the special music on the Fourth of July. As Minister of Music, he saw it as his duty. He gave the choir the Sunday off, and they sat in the pews with their families.

My Uncle Randy was five feet nine inches tall. He had brown hair that was level 8 on the Norwood scale for receding hairlines. He could wear a different Sunday suit almost every week for six months. He was also principal at the local middle school and a coach.

Uncle Randy was always a fireball of energy. After mowing someone else's yard, picking corn for the family and leading the choir, he still had enough stamina to beat his nephews in basketball. We would beg him to unlock the new Sopchoppy Gym for us to play. As payment, he beat us soundly shooting three pointers like Larry Bird. In addition to all these talents, Uncle Randy could play the guitar and carry a pitch-perfect tune. He knew the words to every hymn and with his back to the congregation, conducted the choir's timing with his rhythmic hand gestures.

On the Fourth of July, my Uncle Randy wore his blue suit with an American Flag tie. The congregation struggles to survive morning announcements. After standing for the "Star-Spangled Banner" as the introductory hymn, Uncle Randy bounces to the podium and asks us to be seated.

"I want all my veterans in the congregation to stand back up!" Randy encouraged.

My dad stood up. He did a short stint in the U. S. Army as a medic and a platoon leader before joining the National Guard. My Uncle Dan stands up as well. He did a tour in the U. S. Navy and was on board a ship in the Pacific to witness nuclear bomb testing. Looking around, almost 70% of the men over forty years old stood to be recognized.

After recognizing them for their service, my Uncle Randy asked the congregation to give the veterans a round of applause that "they deserved!" The crowd responded with a thunderous show of their appreciation.

Uncle Randy then took the corded microphone that was under the podium and stepped to the side of the podium. He held it away from his mouth, clearing his throat as the pre-recorded music began to play. What happens next is a patriotic medley like no other. Uncle Randy sings snippets of "Yankee Doodle Dandy", "The Battle Hymn of the Republic" and "This Land is Your Land". He commands the stage, moving about and engaging with the crowd. The music transitions each time. Uncle Randy recognizes all four branches of the Armed Forces with another medley including "Anchors Away" and "The Halls of Montezuma". The finale for this production is "America the Beautiful", and Uncle Randy asks the crowd to stand with him and sing.

After his performance, the congregation stays on its feet and applauds. They clap louder than they had before. Echoes of "Amen" are heard throughout the church. The preacher approaches Randy clapping with the crowd and shakes his hand. He asks for a final "Amen" before beginning to preach his sermon.

From what I remember, there were always two grand recognitions for our Nation's birthday. A secular celebration that included Sheriffs on parade, politicians throwing candy, Nashville acts trying to impress and canoe races. Not everybody knew about the second recognition held at the Sopchoppy Baptist Church and the performance by Uncle Randy. It really was no contest between which tradition made you feel best about your country. It was Uncle Randy hands down.

During his later years, my dad lost all interest in the activity at the City Park. He would go to the parades and watch his grandchildren chase candy thrown at them, but that was about it. He made one final river journey to the park, decades later, but this time it was from the Little House.

The Little House was a small one-story Jim Walter kit-home that was on the Ochlockonee River. My dad and Leona bought it from an old man who was looking to sell. It was a mess! They cleaned the junk out, repaired the walls, refinished the floors and created a delightful vacation home. It was only seven miles from their bigger house on the Sopchoppy River. The Little House was next door to land owned by Bully's family. My dad bought a pontoon boat.

Friends and family stayed for short visits at the Little House. In the winter it was usually quiet, except once when someone reported seeing a naked lady waterskiing down the river. In the summer, Ochlockonee River is hopping. Boats go up and down the river all day. People swam on the other side of the river from the Little House playing their Rap-Country music on the sand bar. We called it ski beach. The people there were mostly from the Tallahassee Boat Club, which was three bends upriver. My dad hated being at the Little House on weekends in the summer because of the loud, sometimes offensive, music.

For a short time. My mom and stepfather Russell also owned a house on the Ochlockonee River. It was down-river from my dad's, on the other side of the Highway 319 bridge. Once, my mom and Russell visited on the weekend of the Fourth of July while my family was staying at the Little House. My dad came up with the idea of he and Russell taking their boats to see the fireworks. The Sopchoppy River flows into the Ochlockonee River. Along the route upriver to the city park, both rivers are wide, deep and have few hazards. It would be a lot easier than the river trip we all remembered from Indian Summer to the park.

Like Independence Day "river trips" from my childhood, the trip on the way to the park was uneventful. Russell had a Hurricane deck boat, and he followed my dad on the one-hour journey. My wife and kids, as well as my sister's family, were scattered between the two boats. It was a pleasant ride on the calm water.

We all enjoyed the music at the park, talked with relatives and had a late lunch. Like the earlier year, we all watched the fireworks from the boats. Following the fireworks we started to head down river, in the dark. The people from the Tallahassee Boat Club raced past us. They were quickly downriver and out of sight.

“We’re not going to fly home like those idiots!” My dad assured Russell.

This time my dad handed me a large spotlight that had a 12-volt plug and asked me to shine it for him to see the river. Russell followed us. Painful childhood memories of our first boat trip from the park returned. Repeatedly my dad gave instructions on how to hold the light better. I tried to shine the light ahead of the pontoon boat to his liking.

Dad navigated us back to the Ochlockonee River. Only getting lost near the Ochlockonee State Park. It was very difficult to see the small cut through that would save us thirty minutes. If I had held the light better, we would have found it sooner.

The trip had gone remarkably smoothly. Once we passed the Ochlockonee River State Park, I thought we were home free. I should have kept those thoughts out of my head.

Russell felt confident in the larger Ochlockonee River, now partially lit by the rising Moon. He went ahead of dad’s pontoon boat with the stronger motor on the Hurricane. Russell pulled the boat up to their dock, beating us there by a half-minute. We arrived there just in time to see my mom trying to get off the boat. She got half her foot on the dock, then disappeared like a magician into a stage with a trap door.

“Mom!” Stacey yelled

At that instant, my dad was coasting to dock, and I jumped from the bow to the dock. I ran to the end of the dock, panicked by my mom's sudden disappearance. In the seconds it took me to get there I heard my mom.

"I'm okay, I'm okay... I just fell", she stated the obvious.

She had fallen straight down, feet first between the boat and the dock. The drop was about five feet, but the water was only three feet deep. We were lucky it wasn't high tide. The soft mud bottom had cushioned her fall. Her sandaled feet were deep in the mud. I jumped into the water to help.

"Mom! You're bleeding!", my sister said, she panicked looking down at my mom from the dock.

My mom's face and neck were bright red. It wasn't blood. She had been holding my sister's nieces on the trip home. Their faces had been painted at the city park, and the make-up had smeared onto my mom. After realizing she had survived the fall, my mom's fear was now fixed on the boats rocking up and down next to her head. I reached up and held Russell's boat back and pushed it to the side of the dock.

As the captains finally gained control of their vessels, I helped my mom walk to shore. Her biggest concern now was the sandals she lost in the mud. After getting her on the riverbank and helping Russell secure his boat. I rejoined my dad and family on the pontoon boat.

"I'll be okay!" she said faking a smile as we idled away from her house.

She would have said that if her arm had fallen off. We all waved as my dad pulled us away. Fortunately, that was the last of our excitement. Our short trip to the Little House and docking was uneventful. My wife and I put our kids to bed and Dad and Leona headed home. We all reflected on how lucky my mom was.

The Ochlockonee River boat journey to the City Park was the last time my dad attended fireworks in person. In his older age, he lost all interest in the activities at the park. Hating crowds, he was reluctant to even watch his grandchildren at the parade.

One Fourth of July, he surprised me. The circumstances had us alone together on the holiday evening, and he asked me if I wanted to see the fireworks. Not believing my ears, he qualified.

"We can watch them at Uncle Roberts", he said.

Of course, I agreed to my dad's proposition. He drove us to Robert's in his GMC truck. My Uncle Robert lived on the tallest hill. When we arrived, my dad pulled into Robert's driveway then backed his truck across the road. He went through the ditch and up an embankment to a fence line. We were on property dad inherited from my granddaddy. My dad turned off the truck. I looked to my right and now noticed two other trucks parked near us.

"Look, there they are" my dad said looking through the windshield into the darkness.

I squinted to look past Uncle Robert's yard. In the far distance, barely extending above the treetops, you could see the fountains of light. Even with the windows rolled down we still couldn't hear the fireworks. We watched the distant light show in silence for several minutes. We saw the pauses in the show and knew that's when the mortars were exploding. Toward the end of the show the final barrage of remaining fireworks was their brightest above the tree line.

"Bill Stevens is going to set the woods on fire again." was my dad's reaction.

Camping By the River

My earliest memories of camping are with my dad. One of the first times, we went with dad's friend Mr. Hodge and his son Little Lynn. Mr. Hodge's name was Lynn also, but my dad just called him Hodge. He was a longtime friend of my dad's and an engineer/inventor. Hodge had already invented the sliding glass door locks that my dad sold door-to-door and a gun rack that could be mounted in your truck's back window without drilling holes. Later he would invent the "Catfish throwing arm and wrist trainer."

My dad and Mr. Hodge wanted to meet up with friends of theirs that lived in the central part of Florida. Their friends had planned a father-son camping trip. We were to meet them at their camp on the banks of the Waccasassa River.

I was very young, around ten years old, and Little Lynn was even younger. I had never heard of the Waccasassa River and didn't know where it was. I was just happy to be with my dad for the weekend.

My dad and Mr. Hodge packed up everything we would need for camping. We took Mr. Hodge's white Volvo station wagon and pulled his small boat with it. It took almost three hours to get from Sopchoppy to the Waccasassa River. Once there, Mr. Hodge backed the Volvo down a ramp to unload the boat. Our fathers got out of the car.

"Where's the damn tent!" my dad questioned Mr. Hodge.

Little Lynn and I waited in the back seat and could overhear.

"It must have fell out, Ed" Mr. Hodge replied annoyed at my dad's accusation.

Cusswords followed as they thought back to where they had last seen the tent. They deduced that the tent had fallen out somewhere between Fanning Springs and the boat ramp. That was over 16 miles of road. Mr. Hodge and my dad got back inside the Volvo, and we drove off looking for the tent.

Retracing our drive back to Fanning Springs, Little Lynn and I were told to search the side of the road for the missing tent. I didn't even know what the tent looked like, but I did what I was told. The Bahia grass on both sides of the road was over two feet tall. The scenery looked the same throughout the entire 16-mile stretch. You could barely see the mailboxes on the side of the road.

On the trip back from Fanning Springs there were more cusswords. It was getting late in the afternoon. There was no sign of our tent. Our dads decided to go ahead and put the boat in the water. We would still meet up with their friends on the river. They would see if their friends had any extra room for us to sleep.

By the time we had the boat in the water, it was dusk. Mr. Hodge steered the boat up the river and we traveled until we found their friend's camp. The camp had two cabin tents set up with lights strung between the trees. They were cooking their supper on a Coleman propane stove. After getting the boat to shore, Little Lynn and I jumped out to find boys our own age. I remember the camp being muddy. There were cypress knots sticking out of the mud.

After a little more than an hour at their camp, my dad told Little Lynn and I, it was time to get back on the boat. We were confused because we thought we were going to camp here. It was now dark. The four of us got back on the boat and Mr. Hodge pointed it in the direction we had come from.

We arrived back at the boat ramp. Mr. Hodge tied up the boat to the adjacent dock, and we all got back on shore.

"We're sleeping in the car." My dad told us, finally explaining our circumstances.

The mosquitoes were biting and there was no reason for us to stay outside any longer. We got back into the Volvo and sat in the familiar tan seats. Little Lynn and I were given a Mr. Goodbar candy bar each for supper. It had peanuts in it, so it was nutritious.

My dad and Mr. Hodge were talking in the front seat. Instead of lamenting about the lost tent, they were talking about their friend's camp. Not only did they not have room for us to sleep, but our fathers thought the camp would flood at high tide. My dad talked about the muddy ground and cypress knots that I also saw. Their friends had balked at our fathers' concerns.

The car windows fogged up. Mr. Hodge and my dad reclined their front seats. Little Lynn and I had to put our legs in between their bucket seats to sleep. We used our door's armrest as a makeshift pillow. Our fathers snored, having no problem sleeping after having drinks with their friends. It was a long night, and I did not sleep very well at all.

At daylight, we got out of the Volvo. It was time to get back into the boat and check on our dads' friends. Mr. Hodge headed the boat in that direction. It did not take long to figure out their fate.

Their tents had an unmistakable water line on them. Leaves and other tree debris were at the top of the line, 8-inches above the ground. My dad's friends were out of their tents.

My dad and Mr. Hodge got out of the boat. Little Lynn and I were told to wait. I couldn't hear the conversation between our dads and their friends, but it was clear we were not staying for breakfast. After five minutes, our dads returned to the boat. We went back to the boat ramp and loaded the boat onto the trailer. Soon we were back on the familiar road to Fanning Springs.

We ate at a small diner in Fanning Springs, before going home to Sopchoppy. This was the first time I remember camping by a river.

My dad bought a second boat one summer. I was 12 or 13 years old. His newest boat we called a Gheenoe. It was made of fiberglass and was a cross between a canoe and a jon boat. You could put a motor on the back, but it was easy to paddle. The bottom of the boat was flat, and the side walls weren't very high.

My dad had first seen this type of boat in Titusville, Florida. We were on a trip to see my uncle, who worked on the space program. The Gheenoe-branded boats are made in Titusville. My dad bought a knock-off called the Happy Traveler, but we still called the boat a Gheenoe.

My cousin David and I enjoyed the Gheenoe. The V-hull boat that was my Grandaddy Scott's was hard to paddle. The side walls were too high, and the boat would not go in a straight line. The chocolate brown Gheenoe on the other hand tracked well and moved more like a proper canoe.

My dad hadn't bought an outboard motor yet. Even if he had, I didn't think David and I would be trusted with it. The Gheenoe gave David and I more freedom because it was easier to paddle farther up and down the river.

When we paddled upriver, we could see the other houses in Indian Summer. They were on the river also and there was a wide variety of construction. The first house after my Uncle Bernie's was an A-frame house. It was triangular and had a deck that overhung the river. We treated this house as a landmark to signify when we are on the river straightaway where my dad's trailer sits.

After the very next bend, David and I saw a live oak tree that was bent sideways. It was on the opposite side of the river as Indian Summer. We pulled in the boat to investigate. The riverbank was steep here and over six feet tall. To reach the top, we had to grab hold of tree roots to pull ourselves up. At the top of the sandy bank our climb was rewarded.

The live oak had two perfect 90-degree bends in it. The tree trunk went straight up about three feet, went sideways for four feet, then straight back up again. We sat at once on the part of the tree that was parallel to the ground. From the tree bench we had a good view of the river.

"Scotty, this would make a great camp." David said looking around the area.

I agreed with him, and we got off our tree bench to explore the area. The sandy salt and pepper colored dirt around the tree was covered in a thin layer of dead brown oak leaves. The ground was flat around the tree for about ten feet in all directions. Beyond that was a ditch with a log going over it. Across the ditch was another flat space that was clear from trees and bushes.

"We should camp here tonight!" I excitedly told David.

We quickly slid back down the bank and got back to the Gheenoe. David and I discussed all the necessary items we needed. We paddled past the A-frame to my dad's trailer. As soon as we got to the trailer, we started asking for permission to camp by the river.

Permission was granted! David and I were so excited. We called his brother Brad, who then called his friend Little Bernard. David went home on his minibike to pack. I stayed at the trailer and did the same thing.

Leona packed hot dogs and buns with a bag of potato chips. Later that afternoon, Aunt Sarah brought Brad, David and Little Bernard to the trailer with their camping gear. Bernard was pronounced "Burn-Nerd", not like the fancy English butler name. He was wiry and as tall as David. He had straight brown hair with a bowl haircut. We packed our equipment and provisions into both of my dad's boats and set off for the fantastic new campsite by the river.

David and I paddled slow so that Brad and Little Bernard could keep up in the V-hull boat. We didn't tell them how easy the Gheenoe paddled. All the way there, David and I told them how great the campsite was that we had found. Going against the tide, it took us thirty minutes to get to the bank with the bent tree.

We tied up our boats to the bank. David and I climbed the steep bank as we had before. Brad and Little Bernard started passing camping gear up to us on the bank. When everything was out of the boats, they climbed the bank to join us.

"Damn, this is steep!" Brad had already started complaining.

"It's not that bad. Grab a hold of the roots." I tried to reassure him.

Brad and Little Bernard slipped a few times, but they finally made it to the top of the bank. Finally, David and I could share this perfect campsite. We showed them the tree bench, the log going over the ditch, and the perfect clearings on either side.

They did not seem impressed. They nitpicked the fact that there was only room for two people on the tree bench. Two people would have to sit on the ground. None the less, we were all here. We would make the best of it. We started unpacking and we set up Brad and David's orange pup tent on the clearing across the ditch.

"Look what I got boys!" Little Bernard exclaimed after pulling a black plastic garbage sack from his duffel bag.

"What's in the garbage bag?" I asked.

"This!" Little Bernard shouted, pulling four "adult" magazines out of the bag.

Mine and David's eyes got wide just looking at the covers. Brad obviously knew what was in the bag and was not phased. We stopped all camp preparations right then. Little Bernard passed each of us a magazine, keeping one for himself.

We all sat in reverent silence on the riverbank, reading the media handed to us. Little Bernard took the spot on the tree bench. He deserved it! The rest of us sat in the dirt. All you could hear were birds chirping and pages flipping. After a time, we exchanged magazines and continued. It started getting dark.

"I'm hungry!" David spoke first.

We all were. It was time to build a fire and cook. With the daylight remaining, it was too dark to read. We gave the magazines back to Bernard and he put them back into the garbage bag. It was agreed that we should keep the books at the campsite for another visit. With our short-handled folding army shovels we dug a hole and buried the plastic bag. We covered the disturbed dirt with oak leaves and twigs, to prevent accidental discovery by others.

We split up to find firewood. We looked for dead logs and limbs laying in the forest around our camp. It didn't take long for us to have a big pile. Brad started the fire. Little Bernard disguised the buried garbage bag hole even more; it was now perfectly camouflaged. David and I cut down palmetto branches. The two of us found four branches that had long stems. Then we cut off the fan-shaped leaves and removed barbs from the stem with our scout knives. Sitting next to the fire, each of us took a palmetto stem and sharpened it to be a cooking stick. We all waited by the fire waiting for red-hot coals to be formed. It was now dark.

We were thankful for the food Leona had packed. I used my scout knife to open the plastic package of hot dogs. Each of us took a hot dog and pushed it onto our own palmetto cooking stick. The hot dogs were roasted over the fire, and they smelled wonderful. I carefully rotated my stick to keep from burning my hot dog. David wanted his black and bubbled on all sides.

We ate our hot dogs and passed around the bag of potato chips. David started cooking his second hot dog. The light from the fire lit up our tree bench and the surrounding area. Beyond ten feet though, it was pitch-black dark. The Moon hadn't yet risen and only two or three stars were out.

"What's that." Brad loudly whispered.

We all stopped talking and froze, our ears perked up to listen. There was not a sound to be heard except for crickets chirping. We went back to our business.

Two minutes later...

"There it is again." Brad whispered softer this time.

We all paused again. This time we all heard it. The bushes and saplings on the other side of the river were moving. We all grabbed our flashlights and pointed them across the river. The four dim flashlights we had were no match for the darkness. You could barely see the bushes next to the riverbank, much less anything that was in them.

We all heard the next sound... Rrrrrooooow!

It came from across the river where we heard the bushes rustling.

"That's a wildcat!" Brad said with alarm.

We listened further...

RRRRrrroooowwww! This time the sound was louder.

"That's not a wildcat, that's Uncle Mo." David said trying to reassure us.

RRRRrrow. The growl was softer this time around.

"Maybe its Uncle Robert. I don't know. I know it's not a wildcat." David repeated his assertion.

Brad was the first to pick up a stick and throw it across the river in the direction of the sound. We all followed his lead. We hooped and hollered to scare the beast, or uncle, out of the woods.

"You better get out of here!" Brad yelled across the river.

We all saw the bushes rustling across the river, but then they quickly stopped. We continued to watch, trying to see any sign of an animal or uncle. We saw neither. The surrounding woods were quiet again, except for the crickets.

Then we heard a hoot owl in the woods behind us, in the opposite direction. Brad took his flashlight and went to the tent. The rest of us sat by the fire. In minutes, Brad returned, carrying his duffle bag.

"I'm not staying here boys. You can stay here if you want!" Brad said.

"If you're not staying here, I'm not staying here!" Little Bernard quickly aligned with Brad.

"Come on guys... You know that was Uncle Mo making those noises." I tried to persuade them to stay.

"It has nothing to do with that." Brad said. "There are fire ants in the tent and I'm not sleeping here."

"I'm not sleeping with fire ants." Little Bernard agreed.

I had no argument. That was it. I looked at David. He had started packing his things. We weren't going to camp anymore. I didn't know what to do. Brad and Bernard had already started down the bank to get in the V-hull boat.

"We can come back for the tent later!" Brad yelled up to us.

David and I started packing our things and put out the fire. Like Brad and Little Bernard, we put what we could in the Gheenoe and started paddling back to the trailer. We quickly caught them with our faster boat.

"That was a lousy campsite anyway." Brad said for all to hear.

"It was. There was nowhere to sit but that damn tree. And I'm not sleeping with fire ants!" Little Bernard was criticizing my beloved campsite also.

We paddled the rest of the way without talking. It didn't take as long to get back. The tide must have been helping us now. The Moon was now out. I was trying to think of what to tell my dad. We all listened, and our eyes scanned the riverbanks for signs of a wildcat.

David and I reached the riverbank in front of our trailer first. I leaped out of the boat, onto the bank, leaving David to tie up the boat. I wanted to be the first one to tell my side of the story.

After getting to the top of the hill, I jerked open the trailer door. My sisters were sitting on the living room couch in darkness, with the TV on. Their faces glowed from the light of the television. They didn't bother getting up.

"Where's Dad!" I asked, the frustration in my voice was obvious.

"He's in his room with mom." Tannye answered.

I stormed through the kitchen and down the hallway. When I reached my dad's room, I quickly opened their bedroom door.

"Dad!! they don't want to camp anymore!" I yelled, starting to explain what happened.

I was frozen by what I saw next. Dad and Leona were dressed for bed. My dad slept only in his boxer briefs. They were sitting at the foot of their bed holding flutes of champagne, getting ready to toast. I saw the open green bottle with the white foil top sitting on the built-in dresser behind them. The cork was there also.

"Boy! Get the hell out of here and wait outside!" My dad screeched.

Leona started laughing.

I went back from where I came. Back through the hallway. Back through the living room where my sisters were still watching TV. Back out the trailer door and into the yard. Brad, David and Little Bernard were waiting for me in the yard.

"What did he say?" David asked.

"He told me to wait outside." I responded.

I was now wondering if he meant outside of his bedroom or outside of the trailer. I'm pretty sure he meant outside of the trailer. We sat around the concrete steps of the trailer, waiting for my dad to come outside. I knew we were in trouble. The image of Dad and Leona toasting with champagne was still in my head.

After about ten minutes, my dad came outside wearing his thin white terrycloth bathrobe.

"Boys, what the hell is going on?!" Dad asked, the glow of the TV shown through as he came out the trailer door.

We all started talking at once.

"Dad, Brad and Little Bernard say they don't want to camp anymore." I said, now exhausted from it all.

"I heard a wildcat in the woods!" Brad explained.

"NO! You didn't, it was Uncle Mo!" David rebutted Brad's story.

"I ain't sleeping with no fire ants." was Little Bernard's excuse.

My dad had heard enough.

"Boys, get in the car and I'll take you home!" Dad told my three friends.

He went inside to get his clothes on. I slowly followed behind him. My sisters were still on the couch but eavesdropped on our conversation outside.

"Ooohhhh, Scotty's in trouble..." They teased me.

"Shut Up!" I yelled back as I went to the bathroom to change out of my dirty clothes.

Dad drove Brad, David and Little Bernard back to their homes in Sopchoppy.

The next day, David came back to the trailer. We got back onto the Gheenoe and went to our campsite. We dug up the garbage bag and looked at the magazines. We had seen them thoroughly before, so we didn't look at them long. We took down the tent and searched the campsite for any other belongings.

After reburying the garbage bag and disguising the freshly covered hole, we loaded up the Gheenoe and headed back to the trailer.

"That was a good campsite, wasn't it David?" I asked him for validation.

"It was Scotty. It was... Mildew will pay for this." David threatened.

We waited for our day to come.

As far as I know, the garbage bag with magazines inside is still buried on the riverbank. We could never find it again.

David and I camped many times on the Sopchoppy River. We had newfound confidence after competing in the Fourth of July canoeing races. The river was even more beautiful when you were miles upriver from my dad's house. During the races, we would scout sandbanks and rock formations where we might camp in the future. With heavy rain regularly and sometimes major floods, the banks of the river seemed to change a little bit every year.

At least yearly, David and I enjoyed the combination of canoeing and camping, starting the journey from the Oak Park Bridge and ending at my dad's house. I could tell that my dad was worried about us on those first couple of camping trips. There were few houses upriver between Oak Park and Mount Beasor. At least in those days. Cell phones did not exist. If we had any emergency, it would be difficult for us to contact anybody. It would also be difficult to get to us.

On the other hand, there was little risk of me busting down the door of his bedroom in the middle of the night. So, I think my dad reconciled that with any danger we might be in.

Like the canoeing races, my dad dropped David and I with the boat at Oak Park Bridge. Instead of David's Mohawk canoe, we took the Gheenoe camping. It could hold all our provisions and was much more stable. We usually took everything we could think of that we thought would make us comfortable. This included a tent, sleeping bags, lawn chairs, a cooler, fishing rods and tackle.

Only once did we deviate from taking all our normal provisions. One fall season we decided to "rough it" and camp like Seminole Indians. On that trip we only took a machete, our pocketknives, a lighter and an Indian blanket that was made in Mexico. We built a lean-to shelter out of saplings we cut down and palmetto leaves. That night turned out to be the coldest on record, the lowest temperature was only 26-Degrees Fahrenheit. Remember we had no internet, the daytime temperatures were in the low 70's. We had no warning it would get that cold.

We chopped on a lighter knot all night long to stay warm. When we exposed fatwood's resin with the machete, the fire would roar. This would warm us up so we could go to sleep. The fire would quickly die down as the resin smoldered over. The freezing cold jarred us awake. One of us had to start chopping on the lighter knot again to reignite our fire. Finally, the sun came up and the temperature rose. We laughed at each other the next morning because our faces were covered with black soot from the smoke.

On a "normal" trip we would load the boat with all our supplies. Doing this after somehow getting the wider Gheenoe down the steep embankment. Unlike the canoe races, my dad waited for us to finish loading the boat and waved goodbye from on top of the bridge. This is how I knew he was worried about us. There were no other canoeists or kayakers going with us. The river was silent. David and I waved goodbye as we headed downriver.

Here, and further upriver, is the most beautiful part of the Sopchoppy River. Dozens of bald cypress trees have bases the size of a car. Their 3–5-foot trunks look twisted and mangled with holes in them. Their roots separate at the base, sometimes going sideways for ten or more feet. Some of the tree bases are even hollow and you would swear an elf lives inside. Surrounding the base of the trees are knobby cypress knees of various heights. They rise out of the tranquil black water like stalagmites.

The riverbanks vary from mud to limestone, to snow white sand. You can only tell the depth of the water close to a white sandbar. Here the tannin-stained water looks tea-colored instead of pitch black. The black river water is like a mirror when calm, reflecting all the cypress, tupelo and live oak trees that line its banks. Sometimes the calm water is only disturbed by black iridescent water bugs streaking across the water's surface. They leave tiny wakes as they glide across in random curves. If you are quiet, you can hear the occasional plop of water tupelo fruits falling into the river.

There was no shortage of campsites on this part of the river. Each one looked better than the last. David and I critiqued them until we found the perfect spot. We looked for the following in a riverside camp: 1) a wide sandy bank, 2) a deep place to fish and swim, 3) palmettos to make cooking sticks and 4) Firewood or lighter knots nearby. Occasionally we'd find a bonus feature like a rock wall, or tree we could jump into the water from, or a babbling water cascade that split off from the river.

Our camping routine followed close to the same pattern as our first riverbank camping trip: pitch a tent, throw the sleeping bags in the tent, collect firewood, swim, fish, start a fire, cook supper, then tell stories until we fall asleep. In the dozens of times David and I camped by the river; the only time we ever heard a "wildcat" was that first time with Brad and Little Bernard.

After waking up with the sunrise, we would break camp, re-load the boat and start the journey home. This was a leisure trip compared to the Fourth of July races. We would straddle the Gheenoe seats with my dad's lawn chairs. These were the familiar mid-century modern lawn chairs made from tubular metal frames, woven nylon webbing and wooden armrests. David put his feet on the cooler. I rested mine on the bow of the boat.

We had to go slow. Our high center of gravity in those lawn chairs made it easy to turn the boat over if we took a turn too quickly. With the river's current pushing us along, we just had to steer the boat. Our hands were free from always holding a paddle, it was time to fish.

We let out the line from our Zebco reels, trolling the river as the Gheenoe moved in the water. Trolling meant something different in those days. We leaned our fishing rods against the boat with thirty feet of line trailing behind the Gheenoe. Our fishing rods were baited with artificial lures. We used either a Beetle Spin or Black Gnat with a No. 2 gold spinner to catch bream. Black and yellow colors were best for fishing in the Sopchoppy River. A fishing lure that looks like small Georgia Thumper grasshopper works well. If there was a "fresh", meaning a lot of fresh water in the river from lots of rain, we would use a bigger lure like a Snagless Sally to catch a bass. When we caught a fish, we threaded a nylon rope fish stringer through its gills and mouth. Our catch drug in the water behind us, tied to the boat.

Tupelo Island was always a favorite stop on the journey. It was usually a great place to stretch, pee, or swim, and it was at the midpoint of our trip. We could lay on the sandbar and rest, not in a hurry to get home anytime soon.

On one trip, Tupelo Island wasn't a great experience. David saw a hornet's nest in the woods and called me to see. The gray paper nest was in a small tree only ten feet off the ground. You could hear the humming sound of the hornets from twenty feet away. Of course, we needed to throw rocks at it. We each looked on the ground to find something to toss. Taking turns, we each continued to miss the nest until we exhausted our supply of rocks. Without thinking, I went to retrieve some of the rocks we had thrown. They were now under the nest. Not a good idea!

The entire swarm of hornets descended out of the nest on top of me. David later said it looked like a black cloud.

"Run Scotty! Run!" David yelled at me.

Remembering my hornet survival skills from Looney Tunes cartoons, I ran as fast as I could towards the river. I could hear the buzzing insects behind me as I ran. I did not look back.

Exiting the woods and running on to the sandbank, the only thing between me and the shelter of water was the Gheenoe. I thought I could jump over it! One of the hornets caught me and I felt the burn of its sting on my back! I leaped from the highest point of the sandbank! and fell squarely into the bottom of the boat.

Seeing me in the bottom of the boat, the hornets must have taken pity on me. That's the only explanation for them not stinging me again. I moaned from the swelling sting on my back and now the bruises on my legs. Lying at the bottom of the boat, I could hear David on the bank laughing hysterically at my predicament.

"Scotty, you should have seen yourself running!" he told me, "That was funny as hell!"

I didn't think it was funny at the time.

After Tupelo Island, the rest of our trip might take a little more effort. Especially if the tide was rising against us. If that was the case, we would stop fishing and just paddle. We still weren't in a hurry, so we paddled slowly. There would be nothing for us to do when we got to my house except unload the boat, clean up and clean fish. Each turn of the river and every house on the bank looked more familiar as we paddled next to Indian Summer. The closer we got to my house, the slower we paddled.

It usually took David and I until mid-afternoon to complete the journey to my house. Often, my dad was outside waiting for us to arrive. Looking back, I'm sure he was worried about us. My dad always looked relieved when he saw us pull up to the bank.

However, the first time he saw us sitting on the lawn chairs with our feet perched up, he just laughed. We even had a makeshift shade structure above our heads, made using the rainfly from our tent. He told us to stay in the boat until Leona could take our picture.

My wife and I like to camp, and we do so often. Unlike David and I, we forgo tents and lean-tos, camping instead in a travel trailer or camper van. Still though, when it comes to finding a place to camp, we are always searching for water nearby. It might be an ocean, lake or stream instead of a river. It may not be as beautiful as the black waters of the Sopchoppy River.

There is just something relaxing about sleeping and cooking next to water. Sometimes when my wife and I are sitting by a campfire and the Moon lights up the water, I'll smile. She will ask me what I'm thinking about, and I'll tell her a funny story about David and I camping by the river.

Outboard Overboard

The first boat I remember us having on the Sopchoppy River was given to my dad by my grandfather, Mister Scott. It was a faded seafoam green, fiberglass boat with a deep "V" hull. It was about five feet wide and twelve feet long. The sides of the boat were over two feet high, and the floor of the boat sloped with the hull. It had bench seats molded into it, with holes running under the seats to let the water drain from one part of the boat to another. On the front of the boat was a small deck space that was just a couple of inches below the metal-capped side rails of the boat.

The boat really wasn't made for the type of water in the Sopchoppy River, although I didn't know that then. It was too heavy and wide to paddle. The river was always flat, without waves, so you didn't need a deep V hull. The boat wasn't really made for the ocean either. It had hardly any flotation in it. The boat was probably better suited for use on a large lake, like Lake Jackson where my grandfather fished, when he was younger.

My dad left the boat in the river, with one end of a rope tied to the bow and the other wrapped around a tree. In Florida, there would be hard rain almost every afternoon in the summer. The boat had to be "bailed out" once or twice a week. Sometimes my dad would bail out the water, but usually it was the child that happened to be standing next to him when he noticed the boat was completely full. Since I was with him the most, I had the opportunity to get the most practice... bailing out a boat.

When the boat was full of water, it didn't sink. There must have been just enough foam inside the bench seats to keep that from happening. In the black water, you would just see the silver rails peeking out of the water, forming the outline of the boat. You had to approach the boat with care. The bank was slippery and steep. The boat would rock and even the slightest movement would tip the boat, allowing more water to come in. This was a delicate operation that needed patience and balance.

I would begin by gently pulling the rope, bringing the boat closer to the bank. I then kneeled on the bank and with one arm holding on to a tree, using my free hand, I reached into the boat, beneath the black water, trying to feel around for the "worm bucket". --- In case you didn't know, a worm bucket is just an empty, gallon-sized tin can used to hold bait while fishing. Once I secured the worm bucket, the bailing could begin. I had to be incredibly careful not to rock the boat, remember any sort of movement would tip the boat and water would spill in from the river. If this happened, I would have to start the whole bailing operation from scratch.

Continuing to hold the tree, I would bail water from the boat. Removing water, a bucket full at a time, until the water level was at least six inches below the boat rails. As my arm got tired, the tin bucket would graze the side of the boat rail as I emptied it. Time to stand up and stretch before my balancing act could begin. Stepping carefully from the bank, I gently put my foot on the small deck, at the bow of the boat. I then perched like a bird on my bare feet. Now, using both hands to hold the worm bucket, I continued to bail water while struggling to keep my balance on the unstable boat.

Once the forward compartment, between the deck and middle seat, was mostly empty I could delicately step back on to the middle seat. It took experience to know when the time was right to do this. The water inside the back of the boat was still lapping at the side rails. Moving back too soon and water would spill in... tipping the boat and dumping you into the river. If the boat flipped, I would need help from my dad or David. Complicating the maneuver was the wet, slippery algae on the slanted floor of the boat. "Slick as owl shit" as my dad would say. I never asked him how he knew the friction coefficient of owl excrement, but after slipping into the wet bottom of the boat more than a couple of times, I knew what he meant.

After I continued bailing and after I had finally reached the back seat, the sweat would be pouring off my body. Water inside would start to equalize on the floor of the boat, and the vessel became a little more stable. At this point, I could bail full force, feet firmly on the floor and both hands holding the worm bucket. Towards the end of this operation, time would seem to slow down. I could no longer get full buckets of water as it shallowed in the bottom of the boat. Each bucket would have less water than the previous scoopful. It was like the riddle that asked how many half-steps there are to the wall? Answer: Infinity! After water was almost gone inside, I considered the job done. There was sense of accomplishment, seeing the boat float high out of the water again.

We had one short, wooden Mohawk paddle and a long wooden oar with a rag tied around it. They were kept on the bank so that they wouldn't float away when the boat was full of water. When I used the boat, I would propel it using the paddle. I paddled on one side of the boat... then the other, taking a step from one side of the boat to the other in between. Trying to make the boat go straight. When my dad was in the boat, he used the oar and "sculled".

He could make the boat go straight and twice as fast. I could never scull very well. Dad did it by resting the oar in an open oar lock clamped to the back of the boat. The rag on the oar would be right up against the oar lock as he moved his hand in a figure eight pattern, twisting the oar with each motion. Like magic he could steer the boat just by varying his stroke. He could let go of the oar and the rag kept it from slipping out of the oar lock.

After a couple of years, my dad bought a motor for the boat at the beginning of one summer. It was a very used, five-horsepower, Evinrude outboard motor. It must have weighed 75 pounds. The motor was the same blue color as our Zenith van. After getting the motor, My Dad announced he would take the whole family for a boat ride "up the river" to Tupelo Island.

As I've said before, Tupelo Island was a huge white sand bank, maybe seventy feet long and twenty feet wide, at its widest, on a low tide. There were two big tupelo trees at either end of the sand bank. Honeysuckle bushes surrounded the area. The plant's sweet fragrance was divine when they were in bloom. Across from the gently sloping bank, the water was deep and perfect to swim in.

After finally finding every boat cushion, ski jacket and orange life vest we had, the family loaded into the boat. Leona had packed drinks for us. As we traveled "up the river" towards the "island", the river narrowed slightly. There were more "stumps". Trees that had fallen into the river lying hidden just below the black water's surface. My dad knew where most of the stumps were.

The boat ride took about thirty minutes. As we weaved around each bend of the river, turtles would slowly roll off their log, plopping into the water. We passed the few houses that were in Indian Summer then. Some we had never seen before. First there was the familiar A-frame house. Then there was partially hidden house with a cable wire rope slide stretching across the river. We passed two little camp huts, which were on the opposite side of the river. It was an adventure!

When we arrived at the "island", I jumped out of the front and tied up the boat. The family played on the sand bank, and we swam before heading back home. This was paradise! We didn't fight with each other. There was laughter. My dad was proud of the Evinrude motor, his new investment.

After many weeks and quite a few trips to Tupelo Island, my dad finally let me pilot the boat. I had to go slow because I didn't know where all the stumps were. If the motor hit a stump, it could bend the propeller. Those are expensive. My dad gave me guidance and always reminded me to check the screws.

The "screws" were a part of the outboard motor's mounting bracket that attached the motor to the boat. They clamped the motor to the boat's transom, the flat back wall of the boat. One screw had a handle that was hinged and shaped like a football, it was easy to tighten. The other screw was missing the handle and usually had to be tightened with an adjustable wrench we kept in the boat. If the screws were too loose, the motor might fall off if we hit a stump. As a safety precaution, a thin, cotton rope was tied to the motor's carrying handle and looped around the boat's oar lock. The rope was always wet.

When it was my turn to drive the family in the boat, coming back from Tupelo Island in the evenings, I would narrate the ride back like the captain of a jungle cruise. We had been to the Disney World's water attraction, and I embellished our trips by pointing out the wildlife and fauna. I held my hand over my mouth like I was talking into an intercom. I told made-up, funny stories about the Indians and early settlers that once lived in the region. It kept the family entertained and they would ask for more.

We came home slowly, the motor puttering and leaving a thin cloud of blue smoke in our wake. I went just fast enough to keep the mosquitoes off us. My younger sisters would often fall asleep on the way home. My dad and Leona might share a glass of wine on the return trip.

Towards the middle of the summer, after the motor's "newness" wore off and after several beverages, my dad told me on the way home that I could take the boat out by myself, if I wanted. I casually replied, "OK" in a voice two octaves above my normal tone.

"Make sure the screws were good and tight and to check them now and again." He reminded me about the motor attachment to the boat.

"Also, be careful of stumps!" was my dad's second caution.

The next morning after my dad and Leona went to work, I called my cousin David and told him the good news. He couldn't believe it! He raced to our house on his minibike. Excited and unable to wait, I carried the heavy Evinrude from the trailer, down the hundred-foot hill, to the bank of the river. The motor was stored outside the trailer on a wooden sawhorse, with a plastic tarp draped over it.

"Dang, this thing is heavy," I said to myself.

The motor weighed well over fifty pounds, and I had to stop every ten feet to rest my arms. I needed David's help to get the motor on to back of the boat. I was only glad we didn't drop it through the floor of the boat. I tightened the screws as my dad had instructed and secured the safety rope. David carried the gas tank down to the boat and I went to collect the boat cushions.

Once we were both on the boat, I connected the black rubber gas hose to the motor and pumped the rubber bulb in the hose, priming gas into the motor. I pulled the choke knob out, put the motor in neutral and pulled on the starter rope. The motor didn't start, so I pulled it again. Then again and again and again. I pulled until my arm got tired, used some cuss words that my dad did, then asked David to give it try. The smell of gasoline permeated the air. David tried pulling on the cord. Still the motor wouldn't start. When he was tired, we both just sat in the boat, defeated, wondering what to do next. I knew I didn't want to carry the motor back up the hill.

After about ten minutes, I took David's place at the back of the boat and reinspected the motor's settings. The only thing we could think about changing was the motor's choke, so I pushed in the knob and tried pulling the starter rope again. After three tries, the motor cranked! Billowing blue smoke on to the surface of the river. We looked at each other excitedly and David untied the boat. I slowly backed us out into the river, put the motor in forward gear and we set out for Tupelo Island. This was my first time going there under propulsion without the rest of the family.

I drove the boat past the nearby A-frame house and the biggest fallen tree in the river. David was in the middle seat, enjoying the ride. We went under the cable slide and past the two camp huts. I periodically checked the "screws" as my dad had instructed. I beached the boat on to Tupelo Island and we tied the rope off. We swam, then laid on the beach chewing on honeysuckle vines, enjoying the peace and quiet. After we became bored, we both regretted not bringing fishing gear and decided to go back home.

On the way back, I retraced my path expertly avoiding stumps hidden in the water and gained more confidence with each river bend that we passed. We picked up speed. Everything was fine. About halfway home when we were both the most comfortable, there was suddenly a loud THUD... as the motor hit a stump. The boat stopped. The back of the motor flew out of the water and the propeller cavitated at the surface. I let off the throttle, shoved the gear shift into neutral and the motor slowly pivoted back down to its proper position.

David screamed out the obvious, "You hit a stump!"

He laughed like a crazy man in an insane asylum. I just prayed that the propeller wasn't bent. I gently put the motor back in its forward gear and slowly started off again. The motor sounded fine, and boat was moving well. I rechecked the screws. We were good!

Again... gaining confidence with each bend, as the river widened and with fewer stumps to worry about, I picked up speed. By the time we passed the A-frame house, we were going wide open. The deep V hull of the boat left a huge wake behind us, and waves of water washed onto the bank's shore. Turtles barely had enough time to get into the water before the waves crashed into them. We went down the long straight away in front of my family's house, wind in our hair. The motor screamed like a race car. No one was in my yard to cheer us as we went by this time.

The fateful day occurred late into the summer. My dad's childhood and longtime friend came by to visit. It was Lynn Hodge. Mr. Hodge the mechanical engineer and inventor. He worked in Tallahassee and later moved to work in Gainesville.

When we were selling his sliding glass door locks, I remember visiting his office in Tallahassee. I admired the large, complicated pencil-drawn schematics on vellum paper. They were on tilted drafting tables with a long parallel bar that could be moved up and down on a string system.

I'm positive this imagery helped inspire me to be an engineer.

Mr. Hodge looked like Mr. Brady from *The Brady Bunch* – during the Hawaii episodes. He had the same tightly wound curls in his silver-blonde hair and had a red-faced suntan.

My sisters and I watched *The Brady Bunch* every afternoon. Mr. Brady's occupation was architect. The metaphors he shared with Mr. Hodge must have given me subconscious motivation later in life.

Mr. Hodge came with his son, also named Lynn. Everybody called his son Little Lynn. My dad and Mr. Hodge at once picked up where they left off. They were good friends and hadn't seen each other in a while.

The last time I remembered seeing Mr. Hodge was at his house on Alligator Point. He challenged my dad to quit smoking with him. It was New Year's Eve, and we were there for a party. My dad and Mr. Hodge each bet that the other couldn't stop smoking. I remember watching them enjoy their last puffs of a cigarette when the clock struck Midnight. They shook hands and Leona said it was time to go home. She took the girls home in the station wagon. My dad and I were left with the Volkswagen.

It would be at least three years before I could get my driver's license, so this would be my first opportunity to drive on the highway at night! Also, my first time using a stick shift! I drove us the 20-mile distance and my dad "helped" me with the windshield wipers. He also helped defog the windshield in front of me, wiping it with his handkerchief. It took us longer than usual to get home, but I did it!

My dad won the bet and rarely smoked a cigarette again.

Little Lynn and I hadn't seen each other in a long time. We both were trying to come up with something to talk about. Little Lynn was a couple of years younger than me.

"Hey dad, can I take Little Lynn out on the boat?" I asked my dad, looking for something to entertain Little Lynn.

He gave me the answer I was looking for, "Sure, Sure... Just be careful! "

I didn't hesitate; in case he changed his mind. I told Little Lynn to come with me to get the boat ready. We carried the heavy motor to the boat, brought down the gas tank and grabbed two orange life jackets. I was in too big of a hurry to get the boat cushion.

While my dad and Mr. Hodge continued to talk at the top of the hill, I cranked up the outboard motor. I now was more familiar with how to use the motor's choke.

"Untie us from the tree." I directed Little Lynn. Giving instructions like an experienced captain.

I idled the motor slowly as I steered us away from the bank. We went upriver at a slow pace as Little Lynn got comfortable on the boat. I took him up the river just a few bends. Then I decided to make a drive-by so my dad could see us. I slowly turned the boat around, avoiding overhanging tree limbs.

"Move up on to the bow and hold on", I instructed Little Lynn.

Little Lynn moved to the very front of the boat. Taking the place of David, he would keep the boat level and help us get on plane, level out the boat and go faster. I rotated the throttle of the tiller and aimed the boat downriver. Increasing the throttle's rotation, we gained speed. The boat was nearly at full speed when we passed my house, Little Lynn waved at our dads who were still busy talking.

We rounded the first ninety-degree river bend, just past my house and the boat leaned into the curve. We were traveling on the first straight away down river and THEN! It happened.

Suddenly, the motor started to pull away from me! The motor was going backward, and the boat was going forward! I held tightly to the motor's tiller, and the motor continued to run! The motor was quickly sideways to the boat, completely off the transom, and I was holding on, as the propeller cavitated the water at full speed! The cola-colored river water churned and looked like fizz from a shaken bottle. The motor bucked in my hand pulled on me like a German Shepard! I couldn't hold on anymore. Visions of the propeller slicing my face, blood spurting everywhere, made me let go!

The motor began to sink. The safety rope! It tightened, the motor gurgled inches below the water. There might be a chance! Anxious half-seconds passed.

Then the thin rotten wet cotton rope broke! The motor's fate was sealed!

The gas tank was pulled into wall of the boat and drug by the gas line, still attached to the motor. The tank lifted momentarily into the air until the gas line disconnected from the force of the motor. The red steel tank clanged back on to the floorboard. I watched, dumbfounded as the motor sank into the black abyss. The motor continued to discharge tiny bubbles as if saying goodbye to me. They were getting smaller and smaller until they went away. All that was left was a thin sheen of gasoline floating down the river.

The river was quiet again.

"What happened Scotty?!" Little Lynn yelled, breaking the silence.

"I don't know what happened!" I screamed back, fighting away tears.

"What did you do?!" Little Lynn asked

"Nothing!" I answered quickly.

"Your dad is going to kill you!" Little Lynn told me reassuringly.

I knew that he was telling the truth.

The rest of the trip, we stayed quiet. Little Lynn took the oar, and I took the paddle as we trekked our way home, lacking any motivation to get there. There was nothing left to say to each other. We finally made our way back up the river to my house. My dad and Mr. Hodge were still on the hill having their conversation. After tying the boat up, we slowly walked up to meet them.

"Hey boy! How was your boat ride?" my dad cheerfully asked, still in a good mood.

"Fine." I said, without emotion.

"What did you do?" he probed, his voice changing tone.

After a short pause, I answered. "We lost the motor…" I couldn't look at him in the face when I said those words.

"WHAT! You lost the motor?! Where!? How?!" my dad now yelling the obvious questions.

"I don't know!" I replied truthfully. "It just fell off!"

"You're going to show me." My dad said sternly.

Mr. Hodge could see that his pleasant visit was now over.

"Ed, it was good seeing you!", he told my dad.

"Lynn, we better get going.", Mr. Hodge motioned for Little Lynn to get in the car.

My dad went into the trailer, took off his clothes and put on his bathing suit, changing costume as fast as a superhero. We went down to the now powerless boat. He asked me how far away the motor was, and I told him it was just around the bend.

"Come on!", He ordered me into the boat.

My dad sculled us down the river to the scene of the crime. He was going fast; we were almost on plane. My dad, standing in the boat, weaving the paddle in the water, looked far into the distance ahead.

He accused me, "You didn't remember to tighten the screws, did you?"

"I did! I did!!! I did tighten the screws!" I cried back. Sounding like the Warner Brothers cartoon character defending his actions.

Once we got to the spot where I think the motor went down, my dad jumped out of the boat into the water. It was now dusk. His milky white skin contrasted with the Coca-Cola colored water. He dove down straight into the water, kicking his feet, disappearing, then he would come back up exhaling his breath with a load whoosh. He'd take three or four short, whistling breaths then dive down again. As the Sun continued to go down, I began to wonder if I was going to lose my dad today also. Then I would be forced to paddle back by myself.

"It's not here" my dad said, breathing hard and hanging on to the side of the boat. "Are you sure you lost it here?"

"Yes." I said quietly, my head down.

My dad climbed back into the boat. It was now dark. We had nothing to say to each other as he began sculling us back home. Neither of us wanted to talk about it the rest of the night. We ate. We went to bed.

The next morning, I woke up and thought I had a terrible dream about the previous day's events, but it was all true. It was the weekend, and my dad took me on his morning rounds through Sopchoppy. At every stop he told everyone that I had lost his motor in the deepest part of the entire river.

"He didn't tighten the screws like I told him to." He repeated to every one of them.

"I did..." I would mumble, under my breath.

The local mechanic, next to Evan's bait store, told Dad he could fix the motor if it was ever found. I think it was Bully that gave my dad the suggestion of dragging a large chain through the river. The chain would hit the motor sending a metallic sound up to the boat, letting us know where the motor was.

For the next week, every evening, my dad took me back on the boat, to the scene of the crime. We dragged the chain through the dark water, Dad diving into the water at the hint of any sound.

"Ssshhh!", he would say, "don't bump the boat!"

I tried to show some enthusiasm for this effort. The mosquitoes were biting. My dad was mostly in the water with his oval black scuba mask and a snorkel. He looked like Jacque Cousteau on an exploratory mission. The mosquitoes weren't biting him. I just wanted it to be over.

I knew the situation was serious when my Granddaddy came with us on the motor hunt. It was a Saturday, weeks after the fateful event. I think this was the only time that I had ever ridden in a boat with my granddaddy. He was always working. Grandaddy had on his blue work coveralls and familiar fedora.

This was going to be the last-ditch effort! We'd find the motor so that normal life could resume or I would live in shame for the rest of my life.

We started looking in the same spot, on the same straightaway, where I had told my dad the motor had gone down. My Granddaddy held the chain. On each faint sound, my dad would jump back in the water. He used borrowed flippers this time, repeatedly diving down like a sponge diver. After several dives, he came back empty. He climbed back in the boat, and we moved further down the river.

"I heard something metal." my granddaddy said.

"What?!" Dad asked?

"I think I heard metal.", Granddaddy repeated.

Dad put back on his flippers and leaped into the water. I lifted my head out of my hands after hearing the first bit of good news. In just a few minutes, after two quick dives, my dad came back to the surface.

"It's there! I found it!" he celebrated.

My dad took one end of the chain and dove down to wrap it around the motor's handle. He came back up and together with my Granddaddy they pulled the motor back up to the boat. I watched as the motor was exposed to daylight for the first time in weeks, water dripping off its cowling. We put it on the middle seat of the boat like it was the golden calf. Dad put his arm around it, tired, as my Granddaddy sculled us back home.

"I knew you didn't know where you lost it." My dad muttered, as we floated with the tide back to the house.

I didn't speak a word. We weren't more than fifty feet from where I said it would be. "Not bad", I thought, considering I could have lost it anywhere between our house and Tupelo Island...

My Dad paid the mechanic to have the motor fixed, and we used it for years after that. It would be another summer before I could drive the boat by myself again.

The Attack on Mildew

My cousins Brad and David Savary were my best friends in Sopchoppy. Their parents are Aunt Sarah and Uncle Buddy. Sarah is one of my dad's younger sisters. They moved back to Sopchoppy from Titusville and for a time lived in a small trailer, before building a house on State Road 22. Together, my cousins and I, made up the Sopchoppy Road Runner Club, named after the Looney

Tunes cartoon character. "Beep! Beep! Zip Tang!" was our slogan.

Brad was the oldest of the three of us. He had a Tweety-bird face with Robert Redford hair. He had blue eyes and was slightly taller than me. When Brad was around, he was the leader. My cousin David and I spent hours trying to persuade Brad to do something adventurous. He would stare off into the distance, stoically, while we pitched idea after idea, until finally we'd say something that would spark his interest. Then he would get a wild look on his face and start helping us formulate the plan. Brad was six months older than I was.

David was the youngest of the three of us and was six months younger than me. He was the crazy one. He had brown hair and was much bigger than me or Brad. David's favorite food was peanut butter and jelly, and he ate it everywhere he went. In fact, that was all he ate. David grew tall fast, and he walked funny because his shoes were always too small for his expanding feet.

When David was younger, he didn't say much. He was kind of backward. As he grew up, he developed a sharp wit. No one could win an insult war against him. If you dare try, he will leave you fumbling for words with everyone laughing at you. David was also an expert in "booger" and "toe jam" jokes. He and I were close, especially as we grew older, and Brad wasn't around as much.

Brad and David's father, Buddy, was a square-jawed, steely blue-eyed, ex-Marine. He looked like the Six-Million Dollar man, but a little crazy. I think that's where David inherited his madness from. Frankly, I was a little afraid of him. I became that way, when we were much littler and we played in the dirt, outside their trailer.

"Where is your new GI Joe that you got for Christmas?" I asked Brad.

"Inside." Brad said.

"Let's go get it!" I said assuredly, standing up, feet aimed at the trailer door.

"Can't." Brad replied.

He continued to play with the few action figures we already had. David was in his other world, doing unnatural things with the bugs on the ground.

"Why not?" I asked.

"Dad's watchin' TV.", Brad told me, still focused on staying outside.

"So...??" I replied, not understanding the connection.

"Dad doesn't like us to get in front of the TV, when he's watching it." Brad explained.

He continued to play. David was oblivious to the conversation.

"But your new GI Joe has the kung fu grip, it has all the cool guns. We can sneak in to where your dad won't notice..." I continued to press.

As I said, this was before I had developed my healthy fear of Uncle Buddy. My dad would let me conduct World War Three in front of the TV. I didn't understand Brad's concerns.

Brad finally paused, intrigued with the thought of kung fu grip, no doubt.

"Well, we could try it... I suppose we wouldn't get in too much trouble going in...But you must be extra quiet. My dad's watching TV, and he won't put up with anything!" Brad laid out his conditions.

Brad stood up and David, now back in our world, followed him. We made our way to the trailer's one and only door. Brad slowly opened it, and the bright sunlight invaded the trailer's dark living room. Brad opened the door only as much as needed and started to crawl in, on the floor. David was right behind him.

They crawled like army men, flat on their bellies, arms and legs out like spiders. Their heads were sideways, facing towards the TV. There was no sound except that coming from the TV. I copied them, thinking this was a game. We slowly, quietly sneaked through the room, towards the back bedroom to rescue GI Joe.

When I was in the middle of the room and my eyes had adjusted to the dark, I could see that Brad had made it to the hallway and was slowly standing up. I continued crawling on carpet, making my way to the safe zone. I decided to slowly turn my head to see what they were afraid of.

There was Uncle Buddy, high above me, his expressionless face and eyes staring at the TV. His face was dimly lit by the blue light coming from the boxy television. This perspective, and my uncle's detached look, gave me the same fear that Brad and David had. I continued my crawl in slow motion, now with more purpose. Out of the corner of my eye, I saw that David had made it! I would be next.

"Heee, Heee, Heee, Heee!". Uncle Buddy burst out laughing suddenly.

It was a strange, crazy laugh, but thankfully it wasn't directed at us. Something struck him funny that happened in the war movie he was watching. I sighed in relief and quickly made it to the safe zone. We gathered in their room and collected the toys we needed.

Brad knew if we went through more than a couple of times, Buddy would yell at us and we'd be in trouble. I don't know what would have happened if we got in front of the TV. My cousins told me I didn't want to find out. We decided to just play quietly in their room and not risk another foray into the living room.

I have a story to describe the difference between my two cousin's personalities and mine. We were in trouble with my Uncle Buddy. I can't remember what we did, but it must have been bad because my uncle was going to spank us for it.

"I'm going to spank each of you until you cry!" Uncle Buddy informed us.

Then he started calling us by name, one by one, from his bedroom.

"Scotty!" Uncle Buddy called for me loudly with military authority.

He knew my name!? I panicked because this was the first time I heard him say my name. I slowly walked through the hall to get to the bedroom.

I suppose I was called in first, because I was the guest. I started crying at once before he ever laid a hand on me. I wasn't used to spankings. With the door closed, Uncle Buddy grabbed me by one arm and drew his hand back to spank me. When his arm moved forward, I wiggled, and my reflexes propelled my butt at the same velocity as his hand. This caused him to barely make contact, and I never felt a thing. I continued to cry, however, in fear that on the next strike I would not be so fortunate.

Uncle Buddy seemed surprised. He didn't think he had hit me, but by the loudness of my crying, he must have. Either because he was frustrated or because I was crying so hard, Uncle Buddy only tried to spank me the one time, and he let me leave the room.

"Brad!" Uncle Buddy called in the next to be disciplined.

Brad went into the bedroom with his head down and Buddy closed the door. David and I heard the whack from the hallway. Brad started crying at once. I continued to sob. David showed no emotion. Brad soon came out of the room. It was David's turn.

"David!" Uncle Buddy called the last of us to be disciplined.

David had the face of a convict on death row walking to the electric chair, knowing what was ahead of him. Brad and I waited in the hallway, both of us still sobbing. We heard the first whack through the hollow door. Then we heard another one.

After a few whack's there was silence; David had refused to cry. This made my uncle even madder! After a couple more whacks, the bedroom stayed silent. This seemed like it was taking forever. David finally walked out of the room. He was red-faced and teary-eyed but never cried. Looking at David's face then up at my frustrated uncle, I could tell that David had won this round.

Over the summers that I spent in Sopchoppy, my cousins and I have had many adventures that I could tell you about. We had BB gun wars in the swamp and on the roof of their house. They had Crosman air rifles, I don't think you really call them toys. I had a Daisy Red Ryder BB gun; it was a toy.

My cousins could pump their rifles up to fifteen times and shoot a bird 25 yards away. My Red Ryder could be cocked only once, compressing a small spring. I had to raise the barrel up in the air when shooting further than twenty feet. My BB traveled in an arc to reach its target. Brad and David's Crosman air rifles could shoot BBs and pellets. A pellet looked like a tiny metal mushroom cloud instead of a ball bearing. It was aerodynamic and larger. A pellet could kill a small animal.

Their rifles held less than 20 rounds, they were stealthy, the only sound you heard was "woosh" as the BB pierced the air, when shot. My Red Ryder could hold over five hundred BBs. They were loosely contained in the hollow tube barrel, and it sounded like a metal maraca when I ran through the woods. When I pulled my gun's trigger, it sounded like Wile E. Coyote jumped on a springboard. I was seriously outgunned, and it was hard for me to hide.

Now when we play war, we always wear the necessary protection. We were warned by our parents, "Don't put someone's eye out!" and we tried to take their advice. We wore at least three layers of clothes, gloves and motorcycle helmets with face shields. Knowing the power of my cousin's rifles, I usually wore an extra layer.

My Aunt Sarah always wondered why she had to wash so many clothes. My uncle wondered why his roof didn't last as long as advertised.

My cousins and I built forts in trees and tunnels in the dirt. We chased our other cousins with roman candles, holding them with rags so they did not burn our hands and remembering to turn them after the first five fire balls. But probably our greatest adventures were tormenting our uncles. Not Uncle Buddy, we were afraid of him. We mainly focused on Uncle Malcolm, Uncle Kenny and Uncle Mo.

Malcolm we were sometimes plain mean to. I do not know why. We once taped him in his trailer, and he had to break the door to get out. During this time, he had the misfortune of living next door to Brad and David. I heard about Brad and David's pranks on Malcolm in my absence. When I was in Sopchoppy, I also took part.

Our attack on Uncle Kenny was born out of my dad's feed store, where I had to work. The hours in the feed store would seem like days. There would be long stretches, hours even, without customers. Thankfully, Cousin David would come by the store, although never on Thursdays. We would entertain each other to get through the hours of boredom.

Thursdays were my worst days in the feed store. That was when the feed truck came to deliver up to 20 tons of feed. The feed was in 25 and 50-pound paper bags. The truck driver would back the tractor-trailer next to the tin shed attached to the store. From inside the semi's trailer, he would slide feed bags, one-by-one to the trailer's side opening. The truck driver looked at my scrawny body and just shook his head. I only weighed 90 pounds. He knew this stop was going to take him longer than he expected.

My task was to grab the bags from the trailer then put them on an industrial cart. When there were three stacks 4-5 bags high on the cart, I would push the heavy cart to the appropriate pile (shelled corn, cracked corn, scratch feed, horse feed, etc.). Then transfer the bags from the cart to the right pile.

There were three rows of feed bag stacks in the storage room, with the path between the rows only 6-inches wider than the cart. I carried a wide roll of wide masking tape with me because it was very common to nick the paper bags with the sharp corners of the heavy cart. I had to quickly jump over the cart and tape the bag before too much the feed spilled out.

With the store being in a non-insulated, non-airconditioned, tin-roofed building, my only relief came from cramming my face inside the narrow door of a refrigerated Coke machine. On these days, I looked forward to a lunch-time dip in the river.

One non-Thursday, I showed David the new cattle prod that had come into the store. The cattle prod had a long white fiberglass shaft with a ridiculously large rectangular battery at the handle and two metal probes on the business end. When you touched a cow with it and pulled the trigger, it was supposed to persuade the cow to move as desired. I showed David this by demonstrating it on his buttocks.

"Ow! That hurt!", David said, squealing and laughing at the same time.

I chased David with the cattle prod, around the store's display shelves. The prod buzzed with each pull of the trigger. Cornered, he wrestled the prod from me and turned it against me. I then discovered how much the cattle prod hurt. After all, they were made to shock through thick cowhide and make a 2000-pound cow run.

"Stop it, stop it!" I screamed for a ceasefire!

After David had extolled his revenge. He agreed to the truce, and I put the cattle prod away. There was only one cattle prod in the store. From that point on we treated it like Excalibur, never to be used in battle again.

Customers were few and far between at the Sopchoppy Feed and Seed. With nothing better to do, David would spend hours with me at the store. Here we planned and schemed our future days and years. We had many "get rich" ideas. One idea was to collect driftwood on the Sopchoppy River and sell it as art. The wood varied in size, and they had hollowed and twisted shapes. We used my dad's boat and collected the floating treasures that were lodged between the tree branches drooping over the river. After many days of collecting, we had a large pile of driftwood on the riverbank, at my dad's house, waiting to be sold. Sadly, we never figured out the logistics of pricing and selling the driftwood. So that idea did not come to fruition.

Our other big idea was to collect blackberries and sell them to Mema and Grandma Kemp. This was genius. We would make a little money and get to eat blackberry cobbler when we went to their house. We spent all Saturday afternoon picking blackberries in the hot sun. By the end of the day, our arms and hands were covered in scrapes and wounds from the sticker bushes we had to reach through to get the berries.

The more we picked, the higher the blackberry price went in our heads. This was hard work! We thought we would easily get a gallon of berries but ended up with less than a quart. After seeing a rattlesnake in the bushes, we stopped picking. We took our haul to Mema's with the expectation of making a sale. Aunt Sarah was there at the time. She and Mema just laughed when we asked for Mema to pay us for the fruit of our labor.

"I tell you what, let me have the berries and maybe I'll let you have some of the cobbler I make." Mema told us laughing her familiar sweet laugh.

David and I decided this was the best deal we were going to get. Our career picking blackberries came to an end.

One Friday at the store, bored as usual, David and I came up with a plan to build tomato launchers. Being a hardware store, we had all the bits and pieces we needed. With no customers, there was plenty of time. We built the launchers out of wood, door hinges, spring door latches, rubber bands, cup hooks and spray paint can caps.

We screwed a door hinge to a 1-inch by 4-inch piece of wood, fifteen inches long. To that we attached a narrow piece of wood with a plastic spray can top at the end. The spray can top would hold the tomato. To provide propulsive energy we attached rubber bands between the rotating board and base, using cup hooks. Stretching out the rubber bands to arm the launcher, a spring door hook and eye latch would hold the launcher in a ready position. We just had to attach string to the hook, hide in the bushes, pull the string. This would cause the hook to release and launch the tomato into the air. Genius!

To us, these tomato launchers were a force multiplier akin to nuclear weapons. They were the first "drones" of modern warfare. Nothing could defeat them. We decided our Uncle Kenny would be the first target.

Kenny was my Grandaddy's brother, Uncle Wilmer's son, and he lived near the middle of town. Kenny looked like a full-sized adult "Ken" doll from Mattel. He had a beautiful wife named Debra. Kenny was an ex-football player. He had short blond hair, was broad chested and walked on pencil thin legs. Of course, he was lot bigger than any of us boys, but Uncle Kenny was nice. He always seemed to be friendly to everyone. We weren't afraid of him.

To join us on the nighttime raid, David and I had recruited Brad and Little Bernard to join the attack. Little Bernard was a wild-eyed fella like David, and he lived in town near Kenny.

Little Bernard was the first person I knew with braces, and their family was the first in the Sopchoppy city limits with a pool. Rumor was that Little Bernard's dad, Big Bernard, even had machine guns. I know he had an airboat. Visions of someone wielding a machine gun in each hand while driving an airboat gave me pause. I had a healthy respect for Little Bernard and his dad.

In the middle of the night, the four of us surrounded Kenny's front doorstep with our remote tomato launchers. Kenny and Debra lived in a brand-new brick house, also with a new pool. We placed our tomato weapons in a fanned-out pattern aimed at the lit-up front door. The front door was between two white columns on a raised brick porch.

Each launcher was armed with an overly ripe tomato. They were expertly disguised to blend into the yard, with sticks and leaves. We laid out the remote trigger strings with one end tied to the launcher's screen door hooks and the other we took with us into the nearby woods. We crouched behind azalea bushes.

Now, with our weapons loaded and cocked, we needed to attract the enemy. David drew the short straw and was chosen to knock on Kenny's door. David slowly made his way to the porch, the rest of us watched. After David was on the porch, but before he could knock on the door, Kenny suddenly opened it.

This caught us and David by surprise! David took off for the ditch beyond the light's reach and dove into the shallow water. Brad, Little Bernard and I pulled on strings to trigger the tomato launch! Nothing happened! The launchers failed! They just sat there!

Kenny heard us, saw our artillery and he ran towards them. Kenny grabbed the tomatoes out of our weapon's spray paint caps and started chasing us. We ran away to Bernard's house to regroup. All except for David, he stayed low in the ditch.

At Little Bernard's, we re-armed with more tomatoes and got on his dirt bike. I was on the back of the bike holding tomatoes in my shirt and one in my right hand. It was no longer a surprise attack. We drove the motorcycle through Kenny's yard three times, me throwing tomatoes at Kenny and missing. Kenny returning fire.

We continued until Little Bernard stalled his motorcycle out directly on Kenny's back porch. Kenny laughed at us and made us get off the motorcycle, then take off our helmets. He smeared the slimy rotten tomatoes on the motorcycle seat and squeezed the tomato juice into our helmets. He told us to put the helmets back on and get on the motorcycle. He laughed. Kenny told us to ride away and warned us never to attack his house again.

After two hours, back at Little Bernard's house, David re-appeared from the swamp. He had branches and cat tails tucked in his clothes. His face had mud on it like a trained sniper. David said he had to hide in the ditch, sometimes seeking refuge in the deeper water. Sucking on reeds to get air. We had to tell him what happened with our attack on Kenny, because he had missed it all.

Our greatest nemesis was Uncle Mo, my dad's younger brother. He was the suspected "wildcat" that scared us when we were camping by the river. It was his turn to pay.

David gave Mo the nickname "Mildew".

David said. "It's the green powdery stuff that's on the back wall of your house, it smells funny, you can't scrub it off and you can't get rid of it."

For my cousins and I, the nickname stuck.

Uncle Mo worked bees with Granddaddy in the summers, so he was always sweaty. He had an oil canned body with skinny arms and legs. His hair was black and straight, parted on one side. We weren't afraid of him because David could throw any insult at Mo's way and Mo would retaliate with only a wry smile.

"You better watch it boy..." Mo would reply with his best comeback.

Our ultimate attack on Mildew was made on a Saturday night. Brad, David and I were bored and there was nothing to do in Sopchoppy. We were younger than 16. We were hanging out near my dad's feed store in the middle of town. A friend of Brad and David's stopped by and told us that he had killed a big oak snake. He was looking for a mailbox to put it, but David had a better idea.

"Let's put it in Mildew's truck!" David suggested with an evil laugh.

We all laughed and came to agreement that this was the snake's purpose in death.

We would put the big snake on my Uncle Mo's truck's floorboard. Uncle Mo was trying to sell the truck, and it was parked near the road, away from his single-wide trailer.

That night, I was appointed as the driver, and I was driving my Dad's Volkswagen Super Beetle. We piled into the car with our friend's dead snake.

My Uncle Mo lived in a trailer on State Road 22, outside of town. He didn't have any neighbors. In the dead of night, we drove towards my uncle's house from the desolate end of the state road, coming from the town's cemetery.

As we crested the hill, laughter and talking stopped. I turned off the car's lights, put the transmission in neutral and shut off the Volkswagen's engine. We coasted down the hill so that Mildew wouldn't hear us. We coasted 50 yards past his trailer, so he wouldn't see the car. Being a dead end, there was never any traffic on this road, so we left the car in the middle of its lane.

As we walked in the dark towards my uncle's trailer, David carried the big snake. Slowly we sneaked into my uncle's yard, our destination being the truck parked near the end of his un-paved driveway. Once there, David opened the truck's door, and the dome light came on.

Suddenly, seventy-five feet away, my uncle's porch light lit up! Mo opened his trailer door and stepped out!

"GET OUT OF HERE!!!" Mo screamed in a mean voice we had not heard from him before!

Uncle Mo was standing on his porch, his pregnant wife Cindy in front of him. Mo was holding a double-barreled shot gun. He raised it up to take aim. We ran away as fast as we could, David dropping the snake.

The four of us ran back to the Volkswagen and we frantically started pushing the car. I pushed with one hand, reaching through the driver's door window, steering the wheel. We knew that if my uncle heard the distinctive sound of the Volkswagen engine, he would know it was us. We pushed the car for probably five minutes. Until...in the far distance... we saw a car coming towards us.

"Don't worry, they'll be going toward Smith Creek." Brad said confidently.

He was reminding us that State Road 22 was a dead end and had little traffic. We silently agreed and continued to push the car.

But the car did come our way! As it got closer, we saw that it had one headlight out.

"Don't worry, the car has one light out... so it can't be a police car." Brad again reassured us.

We were breathing hard now from pushing the car. We continued to push.

We all recognized the distinctive markings of a police car at the same time. I jumped back into the Volkswagen and cranked the car up. The rest piled in through the passenger window without even opening the door. We didn't want the dome light to come on. When I turned the key, the car's rear engine bubbled back to life, breaking the silence. At this point, we didn't care who heard the car.

The cop car passed us. I kept the headlights off, so maybe he didn't see us. Once the police car was behind us, almost to Mo's, I began to drive the Volkswagen like it was the "General Lee" from the *Dukes of Hazard*. I sped away from Mo's, across the bridge towards the Sopchoppy city limits. Everyone else in the Beetle was looking through its small oval rear window.

We all saw the police car slowly turn around. I was paying attention to it in the rear-view mirror.

I turned at the first road on the right and drove the car, lights still off, until we got to the end of road. We saw a partially hidden path along the way. I slammed on brakes and backed the car into the path, far back into the woods.

We stayed in the car, discussing what had happened and the situation we were in. None of us had a driver's license, the police looking for us wasn't Claxton Vause, and Mo could have told the police anything. We all agreed that this was not a good situation.

The car's windows began fogging up. Peeking from behind the dash and seats, we watched police car after police car drive by. It could have been the same police car multiple times, I don't know.

After thirty minutes with no further sightings, we thought the coast was clear. I drove my cousins to their friend's house, and they could walk home from there. Going the back way on Curtis Mills Road, I went back to my house in Indian Summer. This required me to drive on Highway 319, which was forbidden. Once near my dad's house, I glided into the driveway, engine off and lights out so my dad wouldn't hear me get home so late. We all made it home safe.

That night, I didn't sleep well.

The next morning at church, my Uncle Mo was telling everyone about the group of big men from out of town, trying to steal his truck. How he chased them away with his shotgun. He held up my Cousin David's flip flop and remarked how big the SOB must have been.

We could hardly keep a straight face. Fear and laughter were going through our minds.

After a couple of days, thinking the heat was off, I was eating supper with my family, and the phone rang. My stepsister answered, she made a face and said it was for me

.

"I'll pick it up downstairs." I told her and retreated to the basement to have a private conversation.

"Hello?" I asked after I picked up the phone.

"Is this George Scott Strickland?" the voice said with authority.

"Yes, it is." I replied shakily.

"This is the Wakulla County Sheriff's Office investigating a crime. Where were you on Saturday night?" The voice asked.

"Nowhere", I stuttered. "Nowhere... just hanging out with my cousins".

The "Deputy" went on to tell me that he knew that I had driven the getaway car and tried to play a prank on my uncle. He told me that he just got off the phone with my cousin David, who had told him everything. I told him I didn't know what he was talking about, and he threatened me with jail! He said he would be calling again.

I hung up the phone.

I panicked. I later dialed the phone and called my cousins. They told me that Mildew figured it out and that they had confessed. The "Deputy" was actually Uncle Mo, disguising his voice. He had called from my cousin's house. My dad overheard the conversation when he came downstairs.

He blessed me out after I hung up the phone. He told me how much we scared Aunt Cindy, Mo's wife. He told me she was pregnant and that I should be ashamed of myself. He made me go and apologize to Uncle Mo and his wife.

I did.

After driving the Volkswagen back to Uncle Mo's. I sheepishly got out of the car, walked up to the trailer door and knocked. Mildew and Cindy answered the door.

"I'm sorry we scared you on Saturday night", I apologized.

"Boy, I could have shot you" Mo replied.

"I know..." I spoke softly.

"You boys had better watch out, someday you are going to get it. And I'll be there to watch." My uncle threatened revenge.

I reported this to my cousins, and we looked over our shoulders from that day forward.

Mildew's Revenge

On either side of State Road 22, my granddaddy had land. On the right side of the road was his field for growing vegetables or watermelon, his pasture for cows and Mo's trailer. On the left side of the road was Uncle Randy and Aunt Nena's house, which used to be owned by my Aunt Sarah. When the house was owned by Aunt Sarah and Uncle Buddy, the woods and surrounding areas behind their house was me and my cousin's playground.

First, there were the woods right behind their house. This is where we played when we were younger. There weren't many big trees, mostly just bushes and saplings. The clearings between them, however, gave us plenty of room to run, hide and build forts. Our forts were very elaborate. They were dug out of the sandy salt and pepper ground. Sometimes they were a cave and sometimes the roof would be made from sticks and palmetto leaves. We would create fireplaces and shelves in the walls of the dirt. They were big enough for an adult to be in. These forts took us many hours over many days to create, and we were left to our own devices.

Further back into the woods, almost a quarter mile, is Mill Creek. The spring-fed creek winded through large oak and palm trees like a tropical jungle. Vines hung from the trees that we could swing on. The creek had crystal clear water that came out from under a tall, steep hill. The bottom of the creek was snow-white sand, with an occasional black log. When we were close to the mouth of the creek, we would scoop up water to drink and fill our canteens.

We loved swinging on the vines. With our machetes, we would cut the bottom of the one-inch diameter vine from the ground, so that it would swing. You never knew how well you could swing on a vine until you tried it for the first time. Sometimes, you could jump off a hill, hold tightly on to the vine and swing out forty feet, up to ten feet into the air. This prompted the obligatory Tarzan yell from the person taking the ride. Other times, the vine would give at the top of the tree, mid-swing. Then you would land on your butt with spectators laughing at your misfortune.

After out-growing building forts, we mostly played in the area around Mill Creek. It's where we moved our BB gun wars, since we were no longer allowed on the roof of Uncle Buddy's house. It was like having our own private jungle. A jungle means there are animals, and Mill Creek was no exception.

Occasionally we would see a big black snake. We would inspect it from afar to figure out if the snake had a pointed head. If it did, we knew it was a poisonous water moccasin, and we stayed away. If not, then it was a plain old black snake. A black snake is usually skittish, but a water moccasin will stand its ground.

Once we trapped a four-foot-long alligator in Mill Creek, near the Sopchoppy River. We stacked logs on either side of it, blocking its path down the stream. From the two-foot-high bank, we poked at it with the spears we made. The alligator would twist its head back at us and hiss. Getting bored with the gator and not knowing what else to do, we finally left it alone.

The animals we feared most in the "jungle" around Mill Creek were wild pigs. Every so often, when playing around the creek, we would hear their thunderous hooves thumping on the ground. This gave us a very short warning that we either had to run or climb. If they were too close, we had to climb!

We each climbed the nearest tree we could get to. If lucky, there would be something like a magnolia tree close by, which is easy to climb. If not, we would shimmy up a small oak tree sapling like it was a fire pole. When we reached the top of these young trees they would sway back and forth under our weight.

Once high enough in the tree we would watch the passel of hogs, darting between the trees like pinballs. The big ones had tusks coming out of their snouts. Three or four of the pigs easily weighed over two hundred pounds and we were told a pig this size could kill you!

The boars would grunt, and snort and the little piglets would squeal. The herd was always in a hurry. I don't know if they were coming after us or not. We would wait in the trees, sometimes holding on for dear life, until the herd passed us by. It was safe when we no longer heard hooves echoing in the woods.

On the way to Mill Creek was the "Dirt Pit". This was an abandoned borrow pit leftover from when they built State Road 22. Enough dirt had been removed that it left a wide pit with 12-foot side walls. To us, this was another landmark and play area. The walls were too steep to climb with Brad's XR75 motorcycle, but we tried. We would use sticks or shovels to compromise the dirt walls of the pit, narrowly escaping when the wall of dirt crumbled down around us.

The final landmark in the area around Brad and David's house was my granddaddy's pond. "The Pond", as we all called it, was made by my granddaddy. It was on either side of State Road 22 with a culvert running underneath the road. A well was dug into the land to flood the area, thus creating the pond. The larger mass of water was on the same side of the road as Brad and David's house and was over 500 feet across. A smaller part of the pond was on the other side of the road next to Uncle Mo's.

To keep water moccasins at bay, my granddaddy put an alligator in the pond. He found the alligator in a ditch on the way to one of his bee yards. Uncle Bernie was with him at the time. The alligator was only five feet long and my granddaddy thought it would be easy to get him to the pond.

My Uncle Bernie always laughed when telling the story about my granddaddy getting the gator into the back of his pickup truck. The gator thrashing its tail while Granddaddy had it in a "bear hug". My granddaddy had taped its mouth, but the tail was still a mighty weapon. He told about Granddaddy riding in the back of the truck with the gator, rubbing the gator's belly to calm it down. He rubbed the gator's belly for miles, while Uncle Bernie drove the truck. He didn't stop rubbing until the gator could be released into the pond.

The alligator thrived in the pond and got to be good sized. Uncle Buddy told us about seeing the gator lying on the bank of the pond when he was walking by one time. He said that when the gator saw him, it got up on two legs and was chasing him. With the alligator gaining on him, my Uncle Buddy shot it with his 38-caliber pistol. Only stunned, the gator fell on its back and rolled back into the water.

Because of this story and our own experience with the much smaller alligator, my cousins and I had a sense of unease when around the pond. We always looked for the gator when walking nearby.

Surprisingly, with all the exciting areas around my cousin's house, this was not an area that we camped in. I think this is because the house was sold to my Aunt Nena and Uncle Randy. They had two children, Keith and Karla, who were a few years younger than we were. Also, compared to my Aunt Sarah, Aunt Nena was a strict disciplinarian. We knew we wouldn't get away with much when Aunt Nena lived there.

David told me that one time Keith did something he shouldn't have outside of Mema's house and Aunt Nena didn't hesitate. She grabbed Keith's arm with her left hand and started spanking his butt with her right hand. Each "Whack!" coinciding with a pause in her scolding.

"I... Told... You... Not... To...Do... That!... Did...You... Not...List-...en...To... Me!" Aunt Nena yelled as she spanked Keith's behind, each word alternating with a butt whack.

Keith was trying to tell his "Mommy" no, but the words came out jumbled as he screamed a chorus to Aunt Nena's scolding, "Obby! Obby! Obby!"

Keith, barely touching the ground with his feet, ran in circles around Aunt Nena. When she finished his punishment, she turned him loose and found herself dizzy from chasing Keith. She lost her balance and fell into Mema's hydrangeas. David dared not laugh at that particular moment.

When we saw Keith days later, David laughed and mocked Keith's plea to Aunt Nena, "Obby!... Obby!.. . Obby!"

We didn't think Aunt Nena would spank us; we were too big. We decided there was no reason to tempt fate behind her house.

We did occasionally fish in Grandaddy's pond. The pond was stocked with bass and bream. You could catch bream using a cane pole with a cork. My Mema and her mother used to fish there when we had family get-togethers at the pond.

My cousins and I would fish, casting our lures far into the pond. A black Rattletrap worked the best. It wasn't as fun as fishing in the river, unless you hooked a big bass. That didn't happen often enough for me.

I only remember us camping by the pond one time. That summer, Uncle Buddy had given Brad and David a treasure trove. He had traveled out of state and bought boxes of fireworks. The kind that are illegal to buy in the state of Florida. In Florida you could only buy sparklers and Bang Snaps.

I had long had my fill of sparklers. Bang Snaps were only fun as a practical joke. If you're not familiar, Bang Snaps, or Poppers, are little pieces of cigarette paper with sand and silver fulminate explosive inside. They look like a little white berry with paper's end twisted like a stem. They make a loud bang when someone steps on them or if you throw them against concrete. A box of Bang Snaps didn't last very long when I was coping with boredom at the Sopchoppy Feed and Seed.

Far exceeding the firepower of a Bang Snap, the fireworks Uncle Buddy bought were the good stuff! In the four large boxes he brought were Roman Candles, Smoke Bombs, firecrackers, Black Ash Snakes, Fountain Sparklers and M-80s. They brought my cousins and I hours of fun, and sometimes trouble. The fireworks came with no instructions, at least not in English. There was no You-Tube to show us. We had to experiment, and this led us to find many unorthodox uses for fireworks.

Firecrackers were great for exploding fire ant beds. We would push one or more into the mound, light it, then watch the ants and dirt explode into the air. Roman Candles were an excellent weapon. You could wrap the cardboard tube with a rag after they were lit, protecting you from the heat produced, and propel fire balls at your opponent.

You had to count the fire balls as they were expelled, because five balls came out of each end of the tube. After the first five, you needed to rotate the tube in the opposite direction, or you would be shooting the fire balls into yourself. Shooting Roman Candle fireballs at our cousins one evening landed us in big trouble with Aunt Nena.

M-80s were the most dangerous of all their fireworks. We experimented with them in many ways. An M-80 is a small, short, red tube with a green plastic-coated fuse. The tube is filled with 80 grains of flash powder. They were originally manufactured for military use until resourceful people discovered them for fireworks.

A single M-80 could explode open a tin can, sending steel fragments flying. I know, we did it. Instead of watching the ants move through the air, like with a firecracker. A M-80 would obliterate the mound into a cloud of dust.

We discovered the water-proof fuse of an M-80 by accident. David lit an M-80 while the three of us were in an aluminum jon boat, floating on the pond. The first one exploded at the bottom of the aluminum boat, scaring me and Brad to the point of wanting to jump out - except that we remembered the alligator. When David lit the second M-80, laughing at us, we yelled at him to throw it in the water or else. He did.

We watched the M-80 bubble as it sunk to the bottom of the pond. It exploded underwater, its energy pushing a large burp of air to the surface with a splash. A small bream, stunned from the shock, floated to the surface. We had discovered dynamite fishing!

With all our gained knowledge of fireworks use, it was time to invite others to the pond. We invited Little Bernard and George B to go camping with us. Little Bernard had a large canvas cabin tent. All five of us could sleep inside and it was tall enough to stand up in. We all met at the pond and set up camp. We erected the tent in a location near the pond, trying to find a clearing absent of cow pies.

We spent the day showing Little Bernard and George our unorthodox uses for firecrackers and M-80s. Bernard of course was already well versed in firework munitions. His dad had bought him boxes from out-of-state as well. For George, it was all new. After exploding cans, fire ant mounds and doing some dynamite fishing, we settled on just plain fishing with a pole. Brad didn't want to use all the fireworks during daylight. We saved a box and half, storing them in the cabin tent.

After a fun afternoon together, we sat by the fire, cooked, relaxed and told stories. George loved to quote the Euell Gibbons Grape Nuts cereal commercials. He thought it was hilarious.

"Ever eat a pine tree? Many parts are edible," George would quote, then laugh.

"Natural ingredients are important to me," George said five minutes later.

"Tastes like wild hickory nuts." He said when he ate his hotdog.

"David, did you know that a pine bird is edible?" He asked, holding up a pinecone.

"You might not know it, but it is!" he laughed at his own Euell Gibbons impersonation.

George's dad was a wildlife officer, and they lived near the refuge by Ochlockonee Bay. He was used to seeing the tidal influences of the river in his backyard. Because of this he had questions.

"David, what tide do you reckon the pond will be tomorrow morning?" George asked.

"What?" David questioned.

"What tide do you reckon the pond will be?" George repeated, "Is it going to be high or low?"

"George! the pond ain't got no Tide! It stays at the same level all the time!" David explained the lack of gravitational influences on the pond.

"Well, what do you know." George acknowledged.

George wasn't sure if David was kidding or not. We laughed and jokingly said that we might have to move the tent further away from the pond, in case of a "high tide".

After three hours sitting by the fire, it was time to retire to the tent. We had just closed the tent's zipper door when we heard a familiar sound off in the distance...

RRRrraaaooow!

This was a sound that we had not heard since camping by the river, years earlier. We knew that our camp was near our Uncle Mo's and Uncle Robert's houses. Being older now, we didn't expect any trouble from them. We were wrong.

"It's Mildew!", David whispered loudly for all of us to hear.

"I think its Uncle Robert." Brad said – no longer believing a wildcat could make that noise.

"No, it's Mildew here to take his revenge!" David claimed. Reminding us about the night that we planted a snake in Mo's truck.

David partially unzipped the tent door to look out. Holding the door closed to prevent being seen. Likewise, the rest of us each took a window on a wall and peered under its flap, into the darkness. We looked for any kind of movement.

RRRrrrraaaaaooooow!

The "wildcat" was closer, and we thought we knew which direction it was coming from.

"I'm not putting up with this, boys. I'm ready to fight!" Brad warned us of his actions to come.

He reached into a box of fireworks and took out a Roman Candle. He lit the Roman Candle while we were all still in the tent with the door closed. George and I dropped to the floor of the tent, expecting something bad to happen and wanting to stay out of the line of fire.

About this time, the walls of the tent start to collapse. Somebody pulled up the stakes! One by one the aluminum frames that were holding the tent up started to fall on top of us!

Brad, unable to take anymore and holding a lit Roman Candle, stepped up through the tent flap. He stood above the collapsed roof where George, Bernard and I are still enveloped, pushing aimlessly to find the opening. David finds it first and begins to slither out the bottom of the tent's flap.

"Get out of here or I'll blow you up!" Brad yelled into the darkness.

He starts shooting fire balls with the Roman Candle in a fan pattern around the tent. Meanwhile the rest of us begin to follow David out of the fallen tent. We see a shadowy figure disappear behind a small clump of palmetto bushes in the field.

Brad points his Roman Candle in that direction and his remaining fire balls fly within a foot of the bush. David on the other hand is ready to resort to a more primitive form of combat. He picks up a dried-up cow pie and breaks off a piece. He runs toward the bush, throwing the manure pieces into its form.

The five of us are all now outside the tent, yelling into the darkness. Not all of us knew what we were yelling at or where it was. With the element of surprise lost, My Uncle Mo came from behind the bush with his arms held up into the air.

"Alright! Alright! I give! That's enough!" he told us.

David threw one last piece of cow pie and hit him in the chest. Fortunately, Brad was out of ammunition. Uncle Mo now walked towards us and the fallen tent.

"You know you boys had it coming!" He told us.

The excitement started to calm down. We called a truce with Uncle Mo and got assurances that Uncle Robert was not going to attack either. After Mildew retreated into the darkness, all of us but David started re-erecting the tent.

David went to the edge of the pond and washed the cow pie off his hands in the water, being watchful for granddaddy's alligator.

Fishing With Bully

Sopchoppy had a lot of good people living in it. Still does. One of my favorites was my dad's friend, Bully. His real name was Joe, and my dad had known him all his life. Bully's brother Jack was married to my Aunt Jo Ann. Bully worked out of Thomasville, Georgia but spent a lot of his time in Sopchoppy. Everyone in Sopchoppy knew that Bully was an outstanding angler. My dad told me that he used to be a fishing guide on the Ochlockonee River before he started in the road construction business.

When I knew him, Bully was a big man that moved slowly. He didn't get out of his truck if he didn't have to. He looked like an older, bigger version of Sargeant Carter from the TV show Gomer Pyle. He sported the same crew cut hair style. Unlike the television character, Bully talked slow out of the side of his mouth with a distinctive Georgia drawl. His deep voice was sometimes raspy. Instead of Marines, he commanded a road crew.

Bully had a house on the Sopchoppy River also. During the time that I spent my summers in Sopchoppy, his sons David and John lived with him. Bully's wife was named Arie, pronounced "Air – ee". She is probably the sweetest person that I have ever known. Our two families spent a lot of time together. The kids spent afternoons swimming in the Sopchoppy River. The water in the Sopchoppy River is the color of coffee. It's not dirty, it gets the color from flowing through cypress trees. When you stick your hand a few inches into the water, you can't see it. Of course, gators lived in the river, but we were never afraid of them – unless it was dark.

I'll never forget how protective Arie was of little John. He was the baby of the family and didn't know how to swim. He always had to wear a big white Styrofoam bubble with a canvas strap and a metal buckle. Whenever we went to swim, you always heard Arie cry out, "John, do you have your bubble!" I don't know how it kept him afloat without drowning him. I think this type of flotation device was later outlawed. We teased little John, calling him "bubble boy". This was decades before the Seinfeld TV show reference.

Except for me and a few others, Bully had a nickname for just about everybody and everything. He called his middle son David, "Rooster". My cousin Lisa was "Big Eyes", and her sister Katie was "Hurricane Annie". My brother Daniel was called "Stemwinder" and when he was older, Bully shortened it to just "Stem".

Many times, Bully would be talking about someone that I knew, and I didn't even realize it, because I wasn't always familiar with the nicknames he was using. He called mayonnaise, "Gator Milk". Bourbon was called "Loudmouth" because of how you are when you drink it. A typical Bully sentence might sound like, "Rooster! Go take this Gator Milk inside then bring me my Loudmouth from behind the seat of the truck". Everyone that knew Bully knew what that sentence meant.

We never over-planned our fishing trips. My dad would just talk to Bully the night before. Once they decided we would go, we all accepted we would follow Bully's lead. On the morning of the trip, my dad and I would drive all over Sopchoppy getting what we needed. This included the boat, fishing rods, worm buckets, sawdust for the worm buckets, boat cushions for Dad and Bully, life preservers for me and David, gas for the boat, coolers for the fish and beverages, the beverages themselves and ice. We might have to go to four different houses and two different businesses to get everything we needed.

The reason we had to go to so many houses is because there was an accepted "borrow" system in Sopchoppy. No one locked their house or garage in Sopchoppy. If you needed to "borrow" a cooler and knew George Ed had one, you drove by his house, went into the garage and took it. If you saw him later, you might tell him you borrowed it. Because of this, we had to drive all over Sopchoppy trying to reclaim borrowed stuff.

In his cooler, my dad would pack a six pack of adult beverages for himself. In the big cooler there would be a single can of Coke each for me and Rooster. Bully would bring his own Loudmouth. Before fishing we would have to go grunt worms.

Once we finally had the boat in the water and loaded, we would always have to ride in the boat a long way before we could fish. I don't know why. It didn't matter which boat ramp we left from; the fish were always far away from us. The boat was a wooden jon boat. My dad would sit in the front of the boat, in a boat chair, on a boat cushion. Bully sat in the back of the boat, in a boat chair, on a boat cushion, steering the white Johnson outboard motor. The motor had Johnson's red, winged horse on the side of the cowling.

Rooster and I sat on the big Igloo cooler in the middle of the boat. Bully knew every turn of the river and every creek that flowed into it. It seemed like he even knew every tree leaning over the river. After about a half an hour of riding in the boat, Bully would suddenly stop. This part of the river looked like every other part of the river that we had already passed. Once the boat stopped, Bully would declare that we had "reached the first (fishing) hole!" He would tell Rooster or my dad, George Ed to "tie a string around one of them branches". Bully's boat had small ropes positioned all around for this purpose. We would bait our hooks with the worms and drop the bait to the bottom of the river and wait.

We were fishing for bream and the occasional catfish. Bully knew each fish species by name. "That's a nice red belly" or "That's a good stumpknocker", he would say when that kind of fish was caught by one of us. In the winters, we fished solely for warmouth bream. They go to the deepest parts of the river when it's very cold. Bully excelled at finding the deepest holes in the river.

No fish was ever too small to keep.

"Don't you think we ought to throw this one back?" my dad would ask.

"Big enough to make a turd, Ed", Bully would respond.

If the fish stopped biting, Bully would tell everyone to "reel in" and we would untie and go to the next fishing hole. Again, we would stop at a bend in the river under a tree that looked like every other curve in the river and tree that we had just passed.

Bully would know exactly where to stop and catch fish. He would tell me where to "stick my pole" and after following his instructions, I would usually catch a fish. On every fishing trip, Bully would tell the story about my mom's dad, "Mister Scott", getting out of the boat to go to the bathroom and sinking into the wet riverbank up to his thighs. This was a lesson to stand up in the boat and pee in the water if you had to go to the bathroom. With only one can of Coke to drink, I could usually hold it. My dad on the other hand marked every other fishing hole before we departed for another.

Eventually I learned that we weren't in a hurry to get on the river until the tide was right. Bully always said, "First of the rise and last of the fall" was the best for fishing. Which means the fish bite better at the beginning and ending of low tide. Bully taught me to look at the moon to know what the river's tide was. If the bowl-shaped Moon was right side up, then the "bowl was full" and there would be less water in the river. If the bowl was upside down, then the "bowl was empty" and all the water is in the river, thus high tide. The shadow on the Moon changes constantly and white Moon's bowl shape rotates all day. Of course, later, I learned more about how the Moon and Sun's gravitational forces impacted water tides. Bully's Moon bowl trick was an easy indicator.

We would usually fish for six or more hours. The fish went into the same cooler with ice that held my can of Coca-Cola. When we had our sandwiches for lunch, my Coke tasted like fish. I don't recommend it. Dad kept his drinks in a separate cooler by his seat.

Bully would always catch the most fish, even though his "pole" was in the water less than everyone else's. After Bully and my dad felt like we had caught "a mess" and we were out of beverages, it was time for the long boat ride home. Once back, Rooster and I would have "a mess" full of fish to clean.

Dad and Bully would seek more beverages for themselves. Rooster and I would scale the fish using tablespoons on the ricketiest table in the county. Of course, we would count all the fish for bragging rights, then promptly forget the number. My dad or Rooster would clean the catfish using a nail on a wall or tree. Bully would sit down with his drink and start a fire. Arie and Leona would bring all the "fixin's" for hush puppies and cheese grits to wherever we were going to cook.

"Bully, did you catch a mess o' fish?", Arie would always ask.

"We got enough to smear in your face", was Bully's standard response.

If everyone could eat all the fish they wanted, and there was still enough fish to smear in their faces... then it was a "mess" of fish.

My dad and Bully would fry the fish and hush puppies in a hot pot of oil heated over a propane burner. The burner that Bully had sounded like an airplane jet engine. His big round cooking pot was very well seasoned. My dad prepared the fish with flour, salt and pepper by shaking them in a brown paper grocery sack filled with the white powdered mixture. Bully and my dad tested the cooking oil temperature by frying some Hushpuppies first, dipping a teaspoonful of the gooey dough into the oil alternating with rinsing the spoon in a coffee cup of water.

When he was cooking, Bully never had to get out of his seat for anything because Arie was always ready to take him whatever he needed, be it a bowl of hushpuppy dough, cut up potatoes or another drink. Once everything was cooked, our families would feast until they were stuffed. Bully would save the leftover fish for his breakfast. This fishing trip, and the outcome, were repeated numerous times... during my childhood and into my adult years.

On occasion, Dad and Bully took me on hunting trips for squirrels. I was around 12 or 13-years-old. I was armed with my granddaddy Scott's Winchester Model 67 single-shot bolt-action .22 long rifle. It had a knob at the rear of the barrel, just above the gunstock, to cock the rifle. The gun had a rotating safety lever in line with the knob, but I could never remember which position was "safe". Bully also carried a .22 rifle, but his was semi-automatic. My dad used a .410 shotgun.

Once we arrived in the hunting woods, we separated. I didn't see Bully or my dad for at least an hour. I wandered in the woods, heading in no particular direction, looking for any sign of a squirrel. It's funny how all year long you see squirrels playing, running up trees and barking at you – but in the hunting woods, its quiet and there is no sign of them. The only "barking" I heard was my dad in the distance doing his best imitation of a squirrel.

Once, I finally saw a squirrel. I twisted a lever on the rifle to turn the "safety" off. I aimed up into the tree at the squirrel. I fired, holding the rifle at 45-degree angle. Pow!

"Boy, watch where you are shooting that thing!" my dad yelled at me from somewhere in the woods.

After we all meet up, Bully would have four or five squirrels. Dad might have one. I came back empty handed, except for my rifle. Bully and my dad cleaned the squirrels. That evening, Arie would make squirrel and rice.

You must be careful eating squirrel and rice at Bully's house. One night, while sitting by the fire, Leona was sitting next to Arie after helping herself to a large plate of squirrel and rice. Arie glanced over at Leona's plate. Seeing something, she took her fork, reached over and stabbed the meatball shaped object on Leona's plate.

"Bully! I told you to remove the squirrel heads from this batch!" Arie scolded.

Bully just laughed at the shocked look on Leona's face.

Bully and my dad were also avid Florida State University football fans. They had season tickets, sitting next to each other since the 1950's. When I went to the games with my dad, I sat next to Bully. His body covered 1 ½ seats and he sat with legs open wide. I was wedged in pretty good between the two of them.

To me, it seemed like Bully knew every FSU player on and off the field. At one pregame, Bully told me that number

17, from Thomasville Georgia, was going to be the "best athlete FSU has ever had". This was a year before Charlie Ward started in a football game. I later saw his first football start and come-from-behind win at Clemson. Bully was right. Charlie won the Heisman Trophy and was so multi-talented that he went on to play professionally in the National Basketball Association for ten years.

Bully would be sitting in his stadium seat before the players came on to the field to warm up. He didn't leave his seat until long after the game was over, and the crowd cleared. My dad on the other hand pulled us into the parking lot next to the stadium during the first quarter. He always looked for an empty "Golden Chief" parking space, reserved for the largest giving boosters. We parked the Mustang right next to the stadium and made it to our seats by the second quarter. Hating crowds and traffic, we always left before the fourth quarter ended, regardless of the score.

Bully always had bottles of Loudmouth with him at the game, miniature bottles of Early Times Bourbon hidden in his socks. When Bully ran out, Arie had four extra bottles in her socks. She didn't drink alcohol. When Bully needed a Coke mixer, Arie went to get it for him. I can't remember Bully ever leaving his seat at a football game, even to go to the bathroom.

Bully didn't yell at the games. He rarely stood up when everyone else did. He watched the game stoically, taking it all in. He would tell me what to watch for and it invariably came true. When the Seminole games were away, Bully always listened to the games on the radio. Often, that was our entertainment for the fish fry's. Arie though, couldn't bear to listen to FSU football unless the team had a big lead. Close games gave her too much distress, and she blamed herself for the team being behind.

If Florida State's score was far behind the opposing team. My dad and Bully would get in Bully's truck and ride into the "deer woods". The farther behind FSU got, the deeper into the woods they would go, listening to the game on the truck's radio. This was a tradition, because on one trip, Florida State came from behind to win the game. After that, if the Seminoles got behind, Arie would tell them to "go ride into the deer woods."

Later as an adult, staying with my family at the Little House, my dad and I went fishing with Bully and Rooster again. It was after Christmas, and the weather was cool. Rooster and I were now grown and too big to ride together on the middle seat. We would take separate boats, my dad and I in his pontoon boat. He and Bully in the wooden jon boat.

Bully always wore the same thing, no matter the weather or how cold it was. He had a thin white T-shirt covered by an even thinner white cotton collared shirt. His cuffed jacket and pants were dark-blue twill workwear. A very worn black belt and black leather lace-up shoes were his standard. Under the shoes were thin white socks with the elastic failing from carrying too many miniature bottles. On his head was a well-worn ball cap that somebody bought him for Christmas.

My dad avoided the latest technical fashion as well. He rarely wore blue jeans. Always pleated khaki pants and plaid cotton shirts. His undergarments depended on how cold it was. He was not ashamed to wear long underwear if necessary. Depending on the weather, he wore a F.R.M. (Flint River Mills) vest or quilted wind breaker. His trucker cap either said Sopchoppy Feed and Seed or Sopchoppy Tru Value, depending on the decade.

After returning from a successful winter trip catching warmouth bream, we cleaned the catch at Bully's lot, which was next to the Little House. David (Rooster) started a fire. Bully sat in the wooden dining chair next to the fire with a slender stick he used for a cane. A glass of Loudmouth sat at his side. We were warming up by the fire, when Bruce and Bo came by. Bruce was Bully's son-in-law, and Bo (a nickname) was Bully's oldest son. Never in my life have I heard Bo called by any other name. Bruce did not have a commonly used nickname.

Bruce had brought his deep-sea fishing rod. It was a short, stiff rod with large stainless ferrules. The rod blank was over an inch in diameter and the trolling reel looked suitable for catching tuna offshore. I was puzzled about the need for this heavy equipment on the Ochlockonee River.

"Bully, I heard you may have caught some catfish?" questioned Bruce

"Yeah, we caught a few", Bully responded.

"What did you do with the heads?" Bruce asked.

I thought that was weird.

"They're over in a bucket, behind the tree." Bully answered knowingly.

Bruce took the bucket of catfish heads and his deep-sea fishing pole down to Bully's dock. It was late in the afternoon.

"What is Bruce going to do with that rig?" I asked Rooster.

"He caught a gar the other day and they put up a pretty good fight", Rooster replied.

Bruce baited the massive hook that was on a steel leader. He pushed the barb through the six-inch diameter catfish head. Of course, Bully caught the catfish on our trip. Rooster had cleaned the fish using a nail on a tree, peeling off its skin and putting the head in a bucket at Bully's instruction.

Bruce cast his baited line into the middle of the river. Remarkably, the river is over 100-foot deep at the bend near Bully's. Bruce held the fishing rod and sat on a bench at the dock. He was bundled up to stay warm, wearing a ski parka and a toboggan on his head. The rest of us sat by the fire. Except for my dad, he stood with his drink. Rotating his body every so often to keep both sides warm.

Rooster and I put logs in the fire with Bully giving precise directions. He told us what size log and exactly where to put it. The fire was four feet wide, and flames went as tall as my waist. The logs were over a foot in diameter. The fire's embers were white with the gaseous plasma moving in between glowing orange, red, green and blue. The fire was surrounded by big limestone rocks forming a ring. Nobody nourished fire as well as Bully. He was the only man to whom my dad surrendered fire-tending duties.

Bully and my dad's stories were interrupted by the unmistakable sound of fishing reel's drag being tested. The reel clicked slowly. Everyone stopped talking and listened. The tension in the air was like we were on Quint's boat, the Orca, but without the fear of being eaten alive by a shark.

"You got one Bruce!?" Bully asked without looking up from the fire.

"I might" Bruce answered, his Georgia accent ending the sentence with two syllables.

The reel clicks grew stronger, and their speed increased. After a minute of this, there was a constant scream from the reel. By now Bruce was out of his seat. The butt of his rod was in the socket of his rod belt holder. He was prepared for a fight. Rooster and I left the fire and stood on the bank behind the dock to watch. The fishing line disappeared into the water, and it violently moved fifty feet from the dock.

"That ain't no turtle!" Rooster yelled back to Bully.

"Let him tire out Bruce! Don't break the line." Bully calmly instructed staring at the fire embers.

"I won't!" Bruce answered.

The fight went on for over thirty minutes. Bruce was asked if he needed relief, but he did not want help. This was his fish to fight. I was starting to think there wasn't a fish and went back to the warmth of the fire. Then Bruce saw the steel-braided leader come out of the water he called back to Rooster, "Get the net ready!"

Rooster ran to the dock with a long-handled net that had three feet opening. As Bruce continued to reel, he was slowly making progress. Rooster stood on the edge of the dock, the net held in both his hands, ready to attack.

Finally, we saw the head of the beast! With a sudden rush, Rooster swooped the net into the water behind the fish. He pulled the giant animal onto the dock, keeping the hoop well above it for tension.

"We got 'em!" Bruce yelled to Bully

"Well, get 'em on the bank before you lose 'um." Bully finally looked toward the dock.

The fish looked like nothing I had ever seen. It was like a dinosaur with fins. It had a long snout like a crocodile. Tiny sharp teeth protruded from the fish's mouth. From nose tip to tail, the fish was over five feet long. Both Bruce and Rooster had to carry the fish a short distance. Its diamond-shaped fish scales looked like a medieval knight's armor. It was an alligator gar!

"Bo! Get the shotgun out of my truck and take it to Bruce." Bully commanded.

Bo retrieved the weapon from behind the seat of Bully's truck. With its barrel pointed up in the air, he handed the pump-action shotgun to Bruce. The mighty fish was thrashing its body on the bank to get back in the water. Rooster stood guard between the fish and the river.

"It's loaded." Bully calmly said, still sitting in his chair.

Bruce pumped the fore-end of the gun, pointed the barrel at the fish's head and fired. Bang!! Bruce fired a single shot that echoed in the woods behind us and onto the water. The fish no longer moved. Bruce handed the still smoking shotgun back to Bo.

The gunfire explosion made me flinch, even though I knew what to expect. Rooster left his post between the gar and the river and returned to warm fire.

"Scotty, get that axe from behind the woodpile and take it to Bruce." Bully said redirecting his gaze toward me.

Before I could follow Bully's instructions, Bruce came and sat on the bench next to the fire. His face was sweating, and he opened his jacket for some air.

"I got a rest for a minute." Bruce asked Bully for a short break. He was breathing heavy after fighting a fish for nearly an hour, carrying it to shore and shooting it in the head. Sweat was pouring down his red-flushed face.

"We got a bleed 'em out... Rooster come get this axe and take care of it." Bully said, shifting responsibility to Rooster.

Rooster came and took the axe from me. He walked back over to the dead fish and positioned it. He raised the axe behind his head with both hands then swung it down with all his might. He chopped again, then again until he had separated the fish's head from its body.

"Put it on the bank so it will bleed out." Bully told Rooster.

Rooster rotated the fish so that its tail was on top of the sloped bank, its severed neck aimed downward toward the river. He took the fish's head and threw it far into the river. Rooster finally was able to enjoy the fire again. There was a short pause in action, and we all warmed ourselves by the fire.

"Were going to need a Skil Saw to clean it." Bully broke the silence, speaking to the fire.

"I'll get it." Bo responded. He put the shotgun back in its place. He started Bully's truck and drove it away.

Thinking about all that had happened, I laughed at the hilarity of the situation. How many implements are we going to need? I thought.

"You can eat a gar?" I asked incredibly, trying to predict the next steps in the process.

"You can if its real fresh." Rooster answered my question.

We all waited for Bo to get back with the Skil Saw. He finally returned with a handheld circular saw meant for wood. Its casing was made of metal, so it had to be thirty years old. It was made by Craftsman even though Bully was calling it a Skil Saw. Rooster and Bruce retrieved the fish and brought it to the fish cleaning table after rinsing it in the river.

This fish cleaning table was made of wood and consisted of two-by-four boards nailed on either side of two trees. Between the boards was a ¾ inch plywood tabletop cut in the exact trapezoidal shape, resulting from the different size trees. The table was just below chest high and painted battleship gray.

With the gar positioned on the table, Bo plugged the saw into an extension cord. He adjusted the guard above the circular blade exposing ½ inch of saw teeth. Starting just behind the fish's gills, he made his first cut. White fish scales and the resulting dust exited the saw behind the blade, covering Bo's sweatshirt. Bo ignored this and made three more cuts to form a rectangle on the fish's side.

Bully finally got up from his chair by the fire and came up to inspect Bo's progress.

"Get that skin off and cut us out some fillets" Bully instructed.

That was easier said than done. Bo tried to remove the skin from the carcass, but it was stuck like glue. He pulled at the cut section of skin with his hands. Rooster tried as well. Finally, Bo retrieved channel lock pliers from a tool bag in Bully's truck. With the leverage the pliers provided, he was able to remove the skin. The newly exposed meat looked like that of a catfish. I was expecting something completely different from such a strange looking creature.

I returned to the fire for warmth. Bo continued processing the fish, now using a fillet knife. He made more cuts with the saw when needed. After a few minutes of work, Bo made a discovery.

"It's got eggs." Bo told us.

"Wait, you mean we can also have "Gar-viar"?!" I asked, laughing at my pun.

"We better not do that." Bully told me without explanation.

I later looked it up and found that gar eggs are extremely toxic to all animals.

When it came time to cook, Rooster hammered a grill with a stake next to the fire. The grill was homemade using ½" steel rebar. Its cooking surface was a bar bent into a circle with parallel straight pieces inside. A single 1" bar was welded to the circle perpendicular to the grill grate. This part was hammered into the ground. Rooster installed the grill at a height well above the logs, then rotated it over the red-hot embers. Bully sat in his chair with a watchful eye.

Bo placed a deep, cast-iron frying pan on top of the grill and filled it with vegetable oil. We watched as the oil heated until it was glistening. Prior to this, Arie had arrived. She took care of most of the food preparations. She had brought a pot of cheese grits and cut potatoes and Bully waited for the oil to be at the right temperature. She made Bully another drink.

Bully repositioned himself from his wood dining chair and moved over to the bench. Four or five of the fish that we had caught had been put into a large brown paper grocery bag with an inch of cornmeal inside. My dad folded the top of the bag and shook it violently. This coated the fish pieces with meal making them ready for cooking. He handed the bag to Bully along with a pair of short-handled wire tongs.

Bully cooked the fish pieces in the oil a batch at a time. We all sampled fried bream and catfish that we had caught that day. Then it was time to cook Bruce's gar fillets.

"Look, it's still moving." Bo told us he was handing the pan of fish to my dad for cornmeal.

It had been over three hours since Bruce hauled in the prehistoric catch. The fillets had been on ice for more than an hour. I watched with amazement as the meat pulsed on the pan, as if they still had a heartbeat. The meat stopped moving after a short time in the hot cooking oil.

"It tastes like fish, but it has the texture of chicken!" I exclaimed after my first bite of the redneck delicacy.

"Like frog legs", Rooster confirmed.

We stayed by the fire eating fried fish, french fries and cheese grits on thick paper plates. When we finished, we burned our plates and plastic forks in Bully's fire. Bully and my dad were on their third (or fourth?) drink of Loudmouth.

I then made a public proposal to my dad while we sat by the fire.

"You know Dad, as owner of the Sopchoppy Tru-Value hardware store, you should sponsor a Sopchoppy Gar Fishing tournament" I began.

"How many other fish need so much hardware? I mean, today we needed a saltwater fishing rig, a shotgun, an axe, a Skil Saw, a pair of channel-lock pliers and a fillet knife... You could recoup the cost of the prizes selling all the items needed to catch and clean the fish!" I finished.

We had a good laugh at the joke and continued to sit by the fire until the sun had completely set. In the winter, the sky and its reflection on the river were a colorful mix of yellow, orange and red. It was one of the most beautiful sunsets I have ever seen.

We have so many fond memories of being with Bully and his family. My daughters still remember being by the campfire at Bully's and the fishing trips. They will never forget him eating leftover squirrel and rice, sucking on the squirrel skulls before throwing them into the fire.

I have been on dozens of fishing trips with my dad and brother, without Bully. Both before and after Bully's death in 2006. We always talked about Bully and his stories every time we went fishing. Rehashing the same stories about the boat rides, finding fishing holes, about cooking on the bank and the nicknames Bully used. The stories made us laugh, smile, and remember good times. They helped us pass the time when we were waiting for the next fish to bite. If the fish caught was too small, someone always said, "It's big enough to make a turd, Ed."

My dad and I never found the same "holes" Bully had us fishing on. We would always second guess ourselves after tying the boat up to overhanging limbs. Instead of catching fish at every stop, we regularly came up empty. Of course, on our trips we never caught as many fish as we did with Bully.

My dad rarely went to FSU football games after Bully died. My dad remained a Seminole Booster and bought tickets for the next fifteen years. Instead of attending the game, he would let his children or other family members use the tickets. They added police checkpoints to prevent unauthorized access to the best parking spots. The games were no longer worth fighting the crowds according to my dad.

Although he never said it, I sensed that without Bully—my dad's longtime friend and the heart of our fishing adventures—my dad found fishing and going to Florida State football games tiresome. These recreations were now a chore. My dad's old spark seemed to dim because Bully was no longer there to share his knowledge, the old tales, and the Loudmouth.

Vacations In Titusville

Titusville is in central Florida, near the east coast. Three of my dad's siblings used to live there and I remember our family trips visiting them. These were considered our vacations. It took over five hours to make the drive from Sopchoppy. We didn't take an Interstate, instead driving on two-lane highways through small towns like Cross City, Chiefland and Barberville. There were roadside stands selling oranges, grapefruit, pecan rolls and other items all along the way.

Before Walt Disney World opened in 1971, and for a time after, there were smaller theme parks and zoos throughout this area of Florida. On our way to Titusville, we would pass a monkey zoo between Perry and Cross City. In Ocala, there was Six Gun Territory and Silver Springs. Seeing the billboards, we begged our parents to stop at these attractions and occasionally they would.

Titusville itself had the amusement park Tropical Wonderland and a Marine Life Park. Johnny Weissmuller, the star of Tarzan movies, would occasionally be at Tropical Wonderland signing autographs. A short drive away were Playalinda and Cocoa Beaches. Kennedy Space Center was just across the Indian River. In the 1970's the country, and especially Titusville, still had excitement about the Apollo Moon program. Lots of Titusville businesses had space-themed names. Because of its ties to the space programs, Titusville's nickname was the "Miracle City". My sister and I were excited about our trips here.

During the first Titusville trips I remember, Aunt Sarah and my cousins Brad and David lived there. Fortunately, they moved back to Sopchoppy. Otherwise, my time in Sopchoppy would have been very boring. That left my dad's older brother Dan and his oldest sister Jo Ann still in Titusville. We stayed with one or the other during our visits. On our early visits, we always stayed with Aunt Jo Ann.

Aunt Jo Ann was married to Jack Edwards, who was Bully's brother. Uncle Jack was a realtor in Titusville for a time. Really, he was an entrepreneur because in addition to selling houses I remember him farming, owning a vegetable stand, growing worms, even transporting bees out west.

Uncle Jack and Aunt Jo Ann had three daughters, their ages separated by a few years, Bobbie Jo, Lisa and Katie. Katie, the youngest, is a couple of years older than I am. When we stayed at their house, my sister and I slept on the floor of their rooms. We talked all night with our cousins until we fell asleep.

On our excursions, me, my sister and my cousins rode in the back of the small white pickup truck that Aunt Jo Ann and Uncle Jack owned. That's what we did when we went to Cocoa Beach with Mom and Aunt Jo Ann. Cocoa Beach was only 30 miles away. It was a sunny, but windy day when we finally arrived and the ocean waves looked inviting. Waves are much bigger in the Atlantic Ocean than we saw on the Gulf. As soon as we got out of the car and walked on the beach, I headed straight for the shoreline.

I couldn't wait to get into the water. While my aunt and cousins were still setting up blankets on the sand, I was standing at the water's edge, where the waves broke. With no hesitation, I leaped into a wave that was almost four feet tall. It was as tall as I was. That was a mistake. There was instant pain. My chest and left arm felt like a thousand bees had stung me. The wave tumbled me repeatedly. I was in too much pain to stand up. Someone saw me and pulled me out of the water.

The next thing that I remember were lifeguards surrounding my body as I lay on the beach crying. Wearing red bathing suits, they picked up handfuls of coarse sand and rubbed it into the skin of my chest and arm. My aunt, cousins and a crowd of people huddled over me.

"It was a Portuguese Man-O-War!" someone in the crowd yelled.

"I saw it floating in the wave, he dove right into it!" they continued.

I did not know what they were talking about. I hadn't seen anything in the water, other than the wave I dove in to. The sand-coated fingers of the lifeguards were picking what looked like purple spaghetti noodles off my skin. These were tentacles.

"Don't touch it, they will sting you!" the lifeguard cautioned others, giving information that I now knew all too well.

"Here is some vinegar!" another lifeguard said, and they squirted the liquid on to my burning skin using a laboratory squeeze bottle.

Our beach trip was over as quickly as it had begun. On the advice of the lifeguards, my Aunt Jo Ann rushed me to Cape Canaveral Hospital. My sandy body was wrapped in a beach towel when she and mom brought me into the emergency room.

The nurses began wiping the sand off me with wet rags. My chest and upper arm looked like fire covered worms had been crawling all over the skin. In addition, it had been rubbed raw by the shell fragments and sand. The nurses brought out a big porcelain pan and poured a brown liquid into it.

"It's meat tenderizer," the nurse told Aunt Jo Ann, "We found that this works best for jellyfish stings."

I soaked in the meat tenderizer for three hours. I know how long it was because my sister and cousins complained to everyone about having to wait that long in the back of the pickup truck. They were too sandy to come inside the waiting room. They complained about missing out on a beach day. Once I was bandaged up and discharged, we headed back to Titusville.

"What happened!" my dad asked when he saw my wrapped chest.

I just moaned while Aunt Jo Ann retold the day's events. That night I alternated between sitting in front of a box fan or soaking in a warm bath with Epsom salt. There was little escape from the dull pain on my skin. My dad and Uncle Jack retreated to my uncle's houseboat "The Sugar Shack" for a quiet night away, while my mom and Aunt Jo Ann tended my blistered skin.

My cousins brought a book into the bathroom to show me a picture of what stung me. There, on page 47 of the *Seashores Golden Nature Guide*, was the unseen attacker. It had a pink-tipped balloon for a body that floated on the water's surface. Dark purple tentacles extended dozens of feet below the water. The picture showed the tentacles killing a small fish.

After that day, I never forgot what a Portuguese Man-O-War looked like. Fortunately, I didn't have any long-lasting physical scars. The wounds on my chest and arms stayed visible long enough for me to show them off at school.

My dad sometimes would take us on a mini vacation, where he was the only adult on the trip. The first time this happened, my dad and I went to Six Gun Territory in Ocala, Florida. We made the trip in the Mustang, and I was in the front seat! This was my first trip alone with my dad, outside of Sopchoppy. Six Gun Territory was the amusement park that we always drove past on our way to Titusville. I was excited!

The wild west genre was very popular when I was growing up. I remember watching *Bonanza*, *Gunsmoke* and *The Wild, Wild West* on TV. I wasn't a big fan of *Gunsmoke,* like my parents. It had a little too much drama for someone my age. However, *The Wild, Wild West* was one of my favorite shows. The show featured Secret Service agents James West and Artimus Gorden. They were like a combination of Marshall Matt Dillon, James Bond and Sherlock Holmes. The billboards for Six Gun Territory featured the same western themes of the television shows we watched.

Six Gun Territory was as exciting as depicted on the billboards. Behind the giant "fake" mountain at the park's entrance, was a "real" western town. It looked just like Dodge City from *Gunsmoke*. There was a steam-powered train, just like the one featured on *The Wild, Wild West*. There was an "Indian Village" that had "Indians" just like those on *Bonanza*. You could get your picture taken with them next to the teepees.

In the main square of the western town was the Red Dog Saloon. My dad and I watched the can-can girls perform on stage there. Walking around the square were "real" cowboys wearing the hats, vests and six-guns just like on TV. The most exciting part of the day was the "Shoot-out".

The "Shoot-out" happened regularly in town. Suddenly, the cowboys walking amongst you would start eyeing each other. Then one of them would yell at another. The people "just visiting" the town were asked to clear the streets. The Marshall was after the outlaws in town. Surprise gunfire came from the building's roof and from behind. The "Shoot-out" had started!

The cowboys were now behind barrels and wagons taking aim at each other from across the road. Smoke came out of their guns as they fired, and some outlaws were "killed". The drama ended with a duel between Marshall and the fiercest gunslinger. The Marshall always won, and an undertaker came out to pull the dead gunslinger off the street and measure him for a casket.

Seeing my western heroes come to life was exciting for an 11-year-old boy. Getting to see it with my dad made it more special. I was told on this trip that my dad wouldn't be living with my mom anymore. I'm not sure I understood it at the time. I mostly just remembered the "Shoot-out".

On another mini vacation with my dad, he took me, David, Tannye and Stacey to Six Flags Over Georgia

Amusement Park. We traveled in the Mustang on the six-hour journey to Atlanta. It was a long trip for all of us. Either Tannye or Stacey got to sit in the front seat. They alternated between sitting there or in the back seat between me and David. Still no seat belts.

I can't say that I remember a lot about the trip except for three things: 1) the Mustang's under-dash air conditioner froze repeatedly. This required us to turn it off, roll down the windows and let it thaw out. 2) David and I got invisible dogs for a souvenir. This brought enjoyment to spectators during the Fourth of July parades. 3) My dad's college ring.

My dad received his gold college ring after graduating from Florida State University in 1959. The blue stone had a gold inlay "ATΩ", recognizing his membership in the ATO fraternity. On one side of the ring were Florida State University's three torches with the inscription Vires, Artes, Mores (Strength, Skill, Character). On the other is a relief of the Wescott Building. The blue oval stone was displayed prominently half an inch above his finger, sitting atop a mound of gold metal.

Sitting in the backseat of the Mustang, on this trip to Six Flags, David and I learned first-hand about Dad's college ring. It is hard for two adolescent boys to be quiet and good for six hours. Even more difficult if your sister is sitting between you. Because of this difficulty, David and I would test my dad's patience often. When the veil threats of "making him pull over" no longer worked, my dad had enough of our shenanigans.

Dad turned his heavy college ring around so that the stone faced toward his palm. With his left hand still on the Mustang's steering wheel, he was able to rotate his right arm 270-degrees horizontally. With a single swift motion, he thumped David's head with the ring, skipped over my sister's head, and thumped my head with the ring, before returning his hand to the steering wheel.

"Ow!" David shrieked.

"Owww!" I followed.

My sister's laughed.

Knowing now that my dad meant it when he had "Had enough!", David and I sat in shocked silence for the next thirty minutes. Eventually, we grew bored and forgot about the college ring. Rowdiness again ensued or worse, my sister told dad we were poking her.

Thump! Skip. Thump! My dad struck us again.

"Ow! Ha Ha Ha" David and I both reacted to the ring's sting, laughing. We rubbed the fresh knots on our heads.

For the rest of our trip to Six Flags, and on the trip back, my dad played a real-life version of Whack-A-Mole in the back seat of the Mustang. David and I were the moles. David and I tried to predict when we had pushed my dad too far. Ducking our heads to spare them from the college ring's wrath. My dad was more successful than we were. His eyes never left the road.

From that Six Flags trip forward, my dad had a new weapon in his arsenal. One that could settle down mine and David's behavior. We rarely expected the college ring "Thump" from my dad, but we always respected its impact.

During our later visits to Titusville, with Dad, Leona and my three sisters, we traveled in the green Ford Grand Torino. This was before Daniel was born and I got to ride in the front seat between Dad and Leona. Most of the roadside attractions were gone by then. We entertained ourselves having nowhere fun to stop on the way.

During one trip, I entertained myself by wearing a Mortimer Snerd rubber mask and talking like the hick character to my sisters. Mortimer Snerd was a ventriloquist doll operated by Edgar Bergman. The doll's face was like the *Mad Magazine's* "What me Worry" guy. It had realistic skin tones, but exaggerated lips, buck teeth and an elongated nose. The mask was big on my head, so my body and masked face were disproportionate to each other. My sisters were soon bored with my mask and impersonations, but I continued to wear it for hours. Leona couldn't help but laugh at the looks people in cars gave us, seeing this strange little man in our car.

We stayed with Uncle Dan. Aunt Jo Ann didn't have room for all of us. I know that I had stayed with Uncle Dan at least once before, as a toddler with my mom. He reminded me at least once during every visit that I had peed on his brand-new king-size mattress.

Uncle Dan was two years older than my dad. He was bigger and much calmer than my dad. Uncle Dan was Wakulla County's first football player to be offered a scholarship. He played linebacker on the same Florida State Seminole team as Buddy "Bert" Reynolds, who later became a world-famous actor. Lee Corso, from ESPN, was then a coach for the team.

Bert Reynolds' love for FSU was later renowned. The football players lived in a dorm named after him and Mr. Reynolds bought them football pants every year. My uncle told me that during his playing days, Buddy Reynolds was not happy with his playing time at FSU. Uncle Dan claimed he drove Buddy to the Tallahassee airport to leave school for Hollywood. Many years later, we were thrilled when Bert Reynolds' character in the 1976 movie *Nickelodeon*, said he "just got off the train from Sopchoppy."

Uncle Dan lived on Carpenter Road, like many streets in Titusville, named after an astronaut. He had a pool shaped like the state of Florida. Next to the pool was an elevated Lanai. The adults would drink their frozen drinks up there and watch us kids play Marco Polo in the pool. Aunt Sandra was a wonderful and generous cook. She brought us out cheese and meat trays decades before we called them charcuterie boards.

Uncle Dan's wife Aunt Sandra was from Smith Creek, which is a short drive from Sopchoppy. Everyone who knew her recognized her laugh. It was a loud, boisterous, deep laugh with clear pronunciation of "HA, HA, HA, HA, HA!" Almost always five "HAs". When she laughed, everyone nearby turned to see who was so jubilant. She didn't have multiple volume levels for her laugh, just max volume. My Uncle Dan said that someone once tried to steal her purse. He said her "Smith Creek Holler" was so loud and deep that the guy dropped the purse and ran away in fear.

Uncle Dan and Aunt Sandra both worked at Kennedy Space Center. Having good jobs and no children, they treated us like kings during our visits. Uncle Dan had his small plane pilot's license, loved deep-sea fishing, motorcycles and big motorhomes. He was always searching the classified ads for his next "toy". I don't remember riding in any of his toys. I think he enjoyed the search more than using them.

My aunt and uncle gave me posters, stickers and NASA Fact Sheets they had collected from their jobs on the space program. I still have informational posters depicting Saturn V and the Moon missions. During one of our first visits, my dad woke me up at 3 AM to go see one of the last Saturn rocket launches. Uncle Dan would always tell my dad that he didn't think he would have a job the next year. There were frequent headlines about aerospace layoffs. Withstanding the cutbacks, he worked for the same company for 33 years.

With my aunt and uncle's influence, it is no coincidence that my career choice led me to Kennedy Space Center. I finally understood my uncle's job worries when going through the ups and downs of the Space Shuttle Program. Like my Uncle Dan, I worked for the same company for 35 years.

The Walt Disney World Resort in Orlando is only a one-hour drive from Titusville. I think I have been to the resort twice with my dad. On our first trip my parents were still married. We stayed at the Polynesian Resort. The Polynesian and the Contemporary Resorts were the only hotels on Disney property at the time.

The theme park was always crowded and remember, my dad hated crowds. Here, there was no escaping them. In those days, the park limited ride access by giving you a coupon booklet, each coupon designated with a letter "A" through "E". The "E" tickets were for the best rides like the Haunted Mansion and Space Mountain. Once you were out of coupons, you couldn't ride anything. You could buy more coupons, but my dad was happy when our booklets were close to empty.

According to my dad the only fun things in the park were the Jungle Boat and Country Bear Jamboree. They made him laugh. I loved it all, especially The Haunted Mansion and shopping in the "House of Magic" shop. I still have my miniature, glow-in-the-dark Randotti #829 skull.

I was a married adult during my last visit to the Disney Resort with my dad. He "had to take Daniel". This was his only reason important enough to revisit what he considered hell. Leona decided that this time we would go to the new EPCOT theme park. This Experimental Prototype Community of Tomorrow was going to be different, convinced my stepmother. It would be educational!

EPCOT was twice the size of Walt Disney World, and it also had twice as many people on the day we went. Coupon books were no longer used to limit access to rides. All the rides had long lines with waits of an hour or more. This made it a futuristic hell for my dad, instead of the nostalgic one at Disney World. He told us this numerous times in case we forgot.

With my dad's lack of patience, I think we only went on two rides. He enjoyed "Living on the Land" which was a boat ride that showed different farming techniques. The wait was only 45 minutes and in air conditioning.

We aimlessly pushed through the thousands of people, hoping to see a short line to see anything. Leona finally persuaded Dad to go into the Mexican Pavilion located in the World Showcase at EPCOT. After waiting an hour outside its large Mesoamerican Pyramid, just to get inside. My dad was at his limit. Seeing yet "another line" inside the pavilion for "another boat ride."

"Come on!" He yelled, taking Leona and Daniel by the hand, going under a guard rail.

Dad guided us directly to the boat-loading queue, past the 200 people that were standing in line. Before anyone could question us, we were on a boat and floating past the fake volcano. This was the only time my dad smiled all day.

"See, if you hadn't followed me, you'd be waiting for another hour!" he reasoned.

We left EPCOT soon after to head back to Titusville.

Funny, we all still remember having parked in the "Grumpy" section of the parking lot.

Ironically, I moved to Titusville after college to work at Kennedy Space Center and Sopchoppy became my family's primary vacation destination. We were usually there for the week of the Fourth of July and Christmas. This allowed my daughters to experience the same childhood memories of fishing, cooking on the bank and watching Sopchoppy parades.

Worm Gruntin'

Anyone who has heard of Sopchoppy knows about Worm Gruntin'. Remarkably, this traditional method of getting earthworms out of the ground became Sopchoppy's calling card. It all happened because a traveling television reporter named Charles Kuralt reported about the Sopchoppy practice in 1972.

On The Road with Charles Kuralt sought out unusual human-interest stories about americana. Sopchoppy gave him just what he was looking for. His story about the small town showed entire families in the Apalachicola National Forest collecting earth worms. Their method for getting worms out of the ground was to rub iron across a hickory "stob", hammered into the soil. They called it "Worm Grunting".

Mr. Kuralt's two-minute television story focused on the fact that people were incredibly "making a living" grunting for worms. They could make "a couple hundred dollars a week" and the "pay off" was "more than 30 million earthworms a year."

My family joked about the Charles Kuralt piece when it first aired. In those days, nearly everyone in America watched CBS news with Walter Kronkite. So, the Sopchoppy story received a lot of visibility all across the country. Of all the things going on in this small little town, worm grunting had put it on TV. I was already familiar with worm grunting. I had "grunted" for worms with Bully and my dad before almost every bream fishing trip.

In the back of his truck, Bully carried his own stob, which is a broken branch or stake, and part of an old car's leaf spring. Both were well worn from many years of use. There were aways two or three rusty worm buckets sliding around in the bed of his truck. These were discarded large steel cans formally used for beans or coffee. The cans were now half full of damp sawdust dug from where the old sawmill used to be in Sopchoppy, in waiting to be a temporary home for a worm clew. Bully always had all the equipment needed to get worms. You never know when you might need fishing bait.

In the mornings before our fishing trips, we headed for the woods in the Apalachicola National Forest or the bank of my Grandaddy's pond. Earthworms like moist soil. Rooster would be responsible for hammering the stob into the ground. He would start grunting by rubbing the stob with the leaf-spring iron. My task was to look between the twigs and blades of grass for moving earthworms.

You must wait for the worm to get completely out of the ground before picking it up. If you touched the worm when it was only partially exposed, the worm would instantly retract right back into the ground. Bully, looking over my shoulder, made sure I knew this.

When you rub the stob with a piece of iron, it vibrates the ground. Worms can't stand to stay in the vibrating soil. They push their way to the surface to "escape". The noise made sounds like a pig grunting. In Sopchoppy getting worms by this method is called "Worm Grunting" but in other places they call it worm charming or worm fiddling. When I explain the practice to people raised in a city, they always tell me about using electrodes and batteries to get worms out of the ground. As if we were dumb rubes for not carrying a heavy lead-acid battery into the woods and using electricity instead.

On trips when Dad and I fished without Bully, we tried using a wood stake and an axe head to grunt for worms. Our results were never as bountiful as when we were with Bully. Having the right stob and iron it seems are key. I could never generate the same amount of vibration that Bully and Rooster could, even with Bully's equipment.

On a good day, we could collect a few hundred worms in less than thirty minutes. On days when the weather was very dry, we were better off buying worms at Evan's gas station. Worms cost 5-cents apiece back then. What's crazy is they are now selling on eBay or Amazon. Some variations of worms are sold online at the price of $300 for 500 worms. That's expensive fish bait!

The immediate impact to Sopchoppy from Charles Kuralt's story was a small bit of notoriety on national television. Soon after though, there were bigger implications. Local and Federal Government officials start snooping around when they hear phrases like "making a living", "hundreds of dollars" and "30 million a year".

My dad told me the Forest Rangers started patrolling the National Forest, looking for people grunting worms. Internal Revenue Service agents started questioning bait stores about the number of worms they bought and if the money was reported. You couldn't grunt for worms without looking over your shoulder and the fear of interrogation. This drove the professional worm grunters in Sopchoppy underground, so to speak.

Uncle Jack tried to exploit the newfound worm commercialization boon in his own way, by growing them in Titusville. He had a wood structure built above ground that looked like a doghouse with a screened door, built on stilts.

"Why grunt for worms when you can farm them?" Uncle Jack reasoned.

Uncle Jack said worms were more than just fish bait, they were a great source of protein and a benefit to gardens. He researched the many agricultural benefits of worm farming. He even had Aunt Jo Ann try recipes for Worm Pie. Aunt Jo Ann was an excellent cook, but thankfully I never tried her Worm Pie. Sadly, worm farming doesn't make the amount of money or have the same cachet as raising cattle.

In the years that followed, scientists came to Sopchoppy investigating the town's practice of worm grunting. A professor from Vanderbilt University wrote a technical paper for the Department of Biological Sciences. Kennith Catania titled it "Humans Unknowingly Mimic a Predator to Harvest Bait". Funny, I thought the worm grunters knew what they were doing.

Being a scientist, Professor Catania needed to know more. He took measurements of all the grunting equipment used. He used a "vertically oriented geophone" to measure the relative amplitude of vibrations given off from each stroke of the stob. He recorded the vibration amplitudes at one-meter intervals. He charted the Diplocardia Worm quantity and their distance from the stob at the time of ground emergence. His 13-page study concluded that worms came out of the ground because of the vibrations, but there were "still some remaining questions" as to why. There was no mention of partially emerged worms retracting back into the ground if touched, as Bully schooled us.

An article was printed about worm grunting in the magazine Scientific American. They quoted Charles Darwin's 1881 study of moles. The Crothersville Times wrote an article about worm grunting in Sopchoppy. Crothersville is in Indiana. People in Indiana wanted to know how people collected fish bait in Sopchoppy!

Not to be outdone by Scientific American, Popular Science wrote another worm grunting story. They even created graphics for the article to show what a "Stob" and a piece of iron looks like. I mean a "stob" is a pointed wooden stake! Hundreds of vampire movie endings depend on people's inherent knowledge to make wooden stakes! None the less, Popular Science included a picture of a wooden stake in their story to preserve humanity's knowledge of such craftmanship.

Sopchoppy native Gary Revell, I suppose, is the unofficial Sopchoppy spokesperson for worm grunting. He is quoted in the scientific study, Floridana Magazine, The Economic Hardship Reporting Project, The Tallahassee Democrat, CBS News, Modern Farmer, Popular Science...just to name a few. Somehow, Sopchoppy Worm Grunting went viral before that was even a thing.

The Sopchoppy City Commission decided to capitalize on all this free publicity. They proclaimed Sopchoppy as the Worm Gruntin' Capital of the World. They decided the best benefit to the town would be to hold a yearly "Worm Gruntin' Festival". After all, Sopchoppy was well known for its Fourth of July celebrations. This would be another way to attract people to this isolated little town.

The first Worm Gruntin' Festival was held in the 2000th Year of our Lord, 28 years after Charles Kuralt brought Sopchoppy national attention for the practice. The annual festival takes place on the second Saturday of April. Sopchoppy and Worm Gruntin' were now forever linked. It served notice that no other town in the world could be Worm Gruntin' Capital.

The festival committee sells Worm Gruntin' T-shirts, with a new design each year. There is a 500-dollar prize awarded each year for the best design. The first design for the shirt had three "lady" worms coming out of the ground wearing hats, bikini tops and lipstick. Only in Sopchoppy will you see worms wearing lipstick.

Subsequent T-shirt designs depict worms playing music, taunting fish, and heckling worm grunters. A couple of the designs illustrate Sopchoppy worm spokesperson Gary Revell grunting worms. All the shirts show the worms having a good time and feeling positive about being scared out of the ground. The don't even mind being on a fishing hook, except one year in protest the T-shirt worm carried a sign that said, "Eat More Crickets!"

During the day, there are arts, crafts and food vendors scattered about downtown and in the City Depot Park. Since fireworks aren't associated with worm gruntin', it's safe to have the festival in town.

Live music fills the air. Children are given worm gruntin' lessons and prizes are given to the one who grunts the most worms. Gary Revell relocates worms downtown in the weeks before the festival to make sure the new grunters are successful.

There is a ceremony to crown the Worm Gruntin' King and/or Queen. Sopchoppy resident Lossie Mae Rosier was one of the first to be crowned as Worm Queen. She is credited with bringing the practice of Worm Grunting to Sopchoppy and her family was featured in Charles Kuralt's original story about the occupation.

My Mema and her two best friends from school were also crowned one year. I don't remember Mema ever grunting for worms, but she probably did before fishing in Grandaddy's pond.

The yearly celebration concludes with the Worm Grunter's Ball held in the refurbished old Sopchoppy Gym.

Artificial intelligence engines of today's internet tell me it is impossible to count how many stories have been written about Worm Gruntin' in Sopchoppy. They say, "certainly hundreds, and potentially thousands." The topic is in fictional books, on travel blogs and still featured on television like Mike Rowe's Dirty Jobs.

I have been to several Worm Grunting Festivals with my wife and daughters. Everyone loves Worm Gruntin' shirts and outside of Sopchoppy, they're a great conversation starter. The festival is fun, but they don't have a worm parade. For the festival, they put four-foot-tall, wooden earthworm statues in the ground. If you get your picture by them, make sure you're positioned in a flattering way.

Sadly, worm grunting as a vocation is a dying tradition. It seems people don't want to get up early and drive deep into the woods anymore. Artificial bait is more popular. Now you must have a Special Use Permit to collect worms in the Apalachicola National Forest. You can get a free two-week permit to collect about 500 worms for personal use (fishing, worm pies, etc.). To collect worms for profit, you need an annual permit that costs 73 dollars a year. If you are selling worms for the prices on eBay, you might still come out ahead.

Sopchoppy 2025

Taking a tour of Sopchoppy in 2025 is a little different than when I lived there, but the town holds on to the same charm. Leading up to town, the walls of Laurice's gas station are still there. The roof caved in long ago, but the large shade structure that went over top of the gas pump is still standing. The station was used as a set for the movie "Coastlines" in 2002 before the roof caved in. Just down the road, Evan's gas and bait store is closed also.

Just before making the turn into Sopchoppy, there is a new Dollar General. The kudzu-like mercantile store eventually extended its roots into little ole Sopchoppy. It is a good thing it did. The Sopchoppy Grocery, previously known as the Dixie Dandy, closed a couple of years earlier. Dollar General and the Exxon Station are the only two places to buy groceries and beverages.

Ed Lawhon's old "cracker" house is still standing. Having no family members, he passed the house to his good friend, my grandaddy, when he died. My Mema was tired of getting calls about it, so she asked my dad to buy it from her. He paid the assessed value, but a few months later a doctor wanted to buy the house for considerably more. My dad sold it to the doctor and split the profit with his siblings. From the outside, the house looks the same today as it did in 1975.

Going into Sopchoppy, the train depot is now fully restored. The restoration was completed in 2010. It's the only standing depot on the old Georgia, Florida and Alabama Railroad. The Sopchoppy Depot has been made into a museum with old photographs, telegraph equipment and turpentine displays. If it's open, you should check it out.

The city created a park across the street from the train depot. The Sopchoppy Depot Park features a playground, native plants and a walking path that is used for vendors during the Worm Gruntin' Festival.

Just after that, the building that used to be a boarding house is now a recording studio. Tom T. Hall recorded his album *Songs from Sopchoppy* there in 1996. It featured songs such as “St George Isle, “Lost in Florida” and “Redneck Riviera”. Mr. Hall, who’s most famous song is “Harper Valley PTA”, lived in Sopchoppy for a short period.

A better music album about Sopchoppy is *Dirt Road Melodies,* recorded by my cousin Brandon Strickland in 2004. He sings about “Mema and Grandaddy”, “Talkin ‘Bout Fishing” and “Ochlockonee River Blues”, which carry some of the same themes as this book. Brandon is younger than I am, so his experiences came a few years after mine. Judging from his songs, growing up in Sopchoppy within a strong family had many of the same impacts. Brandon and my younger cousins also had their own conflicts with uncle “Mo Bear”, who had evolved from pretending to being a wildcat.

The Fourth of July parade in Sopchoppy is now named after Bill Stevens, the longtime City of Sopchoppy worker who put his heart and soul into the Fourth celebrations. The festivities and fireworks are still at Myron B. Hodge City Park on the River. Park Avenue is now paved, so you won’t get your car dusty on the trip to the celebration. If you go by boat and stay after dark, I recommend you carry a bright spotlight.

The old Sopchoppy Gym was fully restored in 1998. The town uses it regularly for the Worm Grunter’s Ball and musical events. It’s available to rent as a venue for weddings and other events. My cousin David got married there and we held Mema’s 100th birthday party in the Gym.

The post office downtown is no longer open. Longtime Postmaster Majesty Strickland (Maj) retired in 1999. A new post office was built on Highway 319. The Sopchoppy Feed and Seed closed, and my dad built a new store across the street. He and my uncle Mo ran the Sopchoppy Tru Value for many years. My dad still thought of the store as a community service because it never made much money. A realtor is now occupying the building.

As I'm writing this, the two-story Lions Club building is for sale. The club now meets at the Sopchoppy High School, and they still make the birthday/anniversary calendars.

In downtown Sopchoppy, there is now a craft brewery that serves pizza. It's right down the street from the old Feed Store where I used to work. With the strong church presence in Sopchoppy, it took the founder and head brewer Elliot Seidler over a year to convince the City Commission that a brewery was right for Sopchoppy. In 1975, not a single store was allowed to sell any kind of alcohol. It was many years before the gas stations within the city limits could even sell beer. Other than losing the grocery store, my grandparents would probably say this is the biggest cultural change within the city after fifty years.

Four years after its opening, CIVIC Brewing is a now fixture in Wakulla County. It's the only craft brewery in the county. They serve an excellent Tupelo Blonde ale. Next door is the Sopchoppy Bake House and Coffee Company, which makes incredible brownies. Sand and Soul Designs now occupies the building where the Sopchoppy Feed and Seed originally did business. There you can buy ornamental Christmas trees made of driftwood or oyster shells.

I knew you could make money selling driftwood! David and I were well ahead of our time. We just never thought of making Christmas trees.

My cousin Kristin McMillan opened a food store and sandwich shop called "The Loafer's Bench". It is located inside the same storefront, behind the legendary bench where my granddaddy and his friends sat and discussed the weather. She has some of my Mema's recipes framed on the wall. I was lucky enough to get a sandwich made by Uncle Robert there.

While I'm talking about food, I recommend that you pick up a bottle of JB's Sopchoppy Sauce. It tastes good on nearly everything. The late James Burge created the sauce 40 years ago. James lived a few bends downriver from my dad on the other side of the Sopchoppy river. His house was just far enough away from my dad's house so that you couldn't smell a dead gator carcass floating in the bushes. Don't ask me how the gator ended up on the bank across from JB's.

My dad was close friends with James' dad Jimmy. Well before JB created his sauce, I used to see him or his dad weekly. His dad always came by the Sopchoppy Feed and Seed to visit. James and I saw each other when he worked in the Tallahassee post office, and I was a summer intern in a mailroom. James always had a good story to tell.

On the way out of town, on State Road 22 – now a county road, there are tall chain-link fences on either side of the bridge. Why? I assume that too many water balloons had been thrown at too many canoeists. It was common for a daring child to jump off it, or an unlucky child to be thrown from it. The fence was a good idea.

In 2011 Mr. Freeman Pigott, 73 years old, drove his dump truck off the older Sopchoppy bridge. His front tire hit the curb, and the truck went through the guardrail. The truck fell twenty feet and landed upside down in the Sopchoppy River. This was a route he had traveled hundreds of times before. Of course, this story was on the front page of the Wakulla News.

Thankfully, Mr. Pigott was quickly rescued. It took a crane to remove his dump truck. The 70-year-old bridge was closed for weeks and there were fears it would never reopen. This accident was the fear of every driver in Sopchoppy finally realized.

"Did you hear what happened to Mr. Freeman?" my dad called me soon after.

The bridge accident confirmed everybody was doing the right thing by letting Miss Myrtle have her space. What is a few minutes' time going to cost you? It was better to let a driving centenarian safely pass by and both of you can stay out of the river.

Thankfully the bridge was repaired, and it hasn't changed much since 1975. It's still a good idea to let a large truck or 100-year-old driver have their space on the bridge before crossing it yourself.

You no longer take your trash to the dump in Sopchoppy. Like most towns, everybody has a large green trash can that gets emptied by the trash truck every week. It's up to you to figure out how to keep the bears out of the can.

There's nowhere to get your television fixed in Sopchoppy anymore, but that's true, just about everywhere. Besides, with these thin flat-screen TVs, there is no room to put a loaner TV on top while you wait for parts.

According to the Tallahassee ABC television station, Sopchoppy has grown from a population of 426 people to 480 in five years. Curiously, one estimate for Sopchoppy's 1970 population is 460. Like other expanding Florida communities, this has some Sopchoppy residents concerned. There is "a lot more traffic than there used to be". I would guess there are probably fewer underage drivers today.

Meanwhile, the population of Wakulla County has tripled since 1970. On Highway 319, where there used to be no traffic lights on the road to Tallahassee, now there are roughly two dozen.

On the road going into Sopchoppy, the rough oyster shell pavement that was on the surface in 1975 has been paved over with smooth asphalt. All the sidewalks have been repaired. There are now two four-way stops when you travel along Rose Street. In addition, multiple speed humps have been installed on the "main" street, to calm down traffic in Sopchoppy.

Remarkably, the roads going through Indian Summer are now fully paved. There are a couple of dozen new houses in the development, mostly on the inland roads. With a major flood every decade or so, the homes on riverfront lots are often re-sold. Last I checked, the A-frame house was still there.

Like Sopchoppy, there have been a lot of changes for me in the last fifty years. After graduating from high school, I moved away from Berea, Kentucky and my summer trips to Sopchoppy, Florida ended.

My stepfather's Ford dealership survived the high interest rates of the early 1980's but was given an ultimatum. The banks wanted evidence of the dealership's solvency, so they asked for a huge sum of money. This resulted in our dealership, like many others in small towns, to close the business. Coinciding with my Senior year in high school my stepfather, Russell, moved to Brooksville, Florida to start a new dry-cleaning business.

In weeks and days leading up to my graduation, my mom and Russell closed the Ford dealership, sold the farm we lived on, auctioned off our farm equipment and had multiple garage sales. On the last full day in our short-term rental house, my mom sold the tea glass right out of my hand. The lady at my mom's garage sale wanted the complete set.

Dad, Leona and my stepsisters came to Berea for my graduation. The next week my mom drove to Brooksville with Stacey, and I drove the Mustang back to Sopchoppy. My plan was to study engineering after graduating from high school.

"Are you going to give up all of your friends just to be an engineer?" Bully asked me.

I assured him that I wasn't. The University of Florida was known for its engineering school and was Florida State University's chief rival. I instead went to Florida State, who just resurrected their engineering program. This after all was my dad and Uncle Dan's alma mater. I never dreamed of going to any other school. Going to college at FSU allowed me to live with my dad in Sopchoppy after high school.

Tannye took over at the Feed Store for a couple of years. I instead worked in Tallahassee. With her looks, Tannye was able to get more help unloading the feed trucks and with getting heavy feed bags into the customer's trucks.

Living full-time in Sopchoppy and attending college in Tallahassee was very different from my earlier care-free summers. The first two years, I carpooled with Little Bernard and others to college. Attending classes and studying long hours to barely pass calculus, chemistry and physics, college took up all my free time. I also attended classes in the summer and didn't have much time for camping or canoe races.

When I started taking engineering classes in my third year, I didn't even have time to carpool. For a couple of semesters, I stayed with my Uncle Buddy and Brad for a couple of nights a week. Uncle Buddy was now pretty mellow and he had the finest big projection screen television available and this new service called Home Box Office. I finally moved to Tallahassee and lived in a duplex with my cousin David near FSU campus. I met my wife-to-be, Lisa, while working part-time in my junior year. Aunt Jo Ann sang The Lord's Prayer at our wedding in Tallahassee.

After graduating with an engineering degree, I was lucky to get a job at the Kennedy Space Center. I moved to Titusville, Florida and my Uncle Dan and Aunt Sandra took me under their wing. Within a year, Uncle Jack and Aunt Jo Ann moved back to Sopchoppy. Their three daughters soon followed them. Uncle Dan and Aunt Sandra moved to Sopchoppy after they retired.

With our two daughters, Lisa and I regularly visited Sopchoppy. We spent a week in the summers and alternated Christmases there. We were fortunate to stay at the Little House. This allowed us to visit my dad and stepmother, without them being subjected to the chaos of young children. My dad always went through a cycle of happiness and grumpiness during these visits. He seemed happiest on the day we left to go home.

"We're happy to see you come and happy to see you go." He told me with a smile on his face.

My daughters got the opportunity to play with their cousins in a jon boat and the old "Gheenoe" on the Sopchoppy River. They jumped out of the tupelo tree and swung on the rope in Honeysuckle Heaven. They dashed for candy at the Fourth of July parades and saw the fireworks at the park. Sometimes they rode on the volunteer firetruck in the parade.

At the end of one summer trip at the Little House my wife and I discussed how much fun we and the girls had on our vacation. We marveled at the money we saved by staying at my dad's Little House. The next day our gimpy-legged miniature dachshund named "Lucky" was bitten by a pigmy rattlesnake on the Little House's back porch. Two days at the veterinarian and 600 dollars later our dog and vacation were saved. It turned out to be one of our most expensive trips.

Regardless of the risks to our lucky dog, we continued to vacation in Sopchoppy. During these years my daughters and I fished with my dad and his friend Bully. We had fish fries after "catching a mess" of bream. We had campfires by the river on New Year's Eves. My kids rang in the new year banging on pots and pans.

My mom and stepfather still live in Brooksville. People are amazed when I tell them how well my parents got along after their divorce. I'm sure it was sometimes strained, but they always did what was best for my sister and me. My stepfather Russell, Dad and Bobby Jack celebrated their 70th birthday together in the mountains. All my parents came to Family Days at Kennedy Space Center to see where I worked and what we created. My parents have been married to my stepparents for nearly half a century.

I kept the Mustang until my daughters were toddlers. After sitting in my garage for over a year, I decided it was time to sell the car. It wouldn't start. I wasn't motivated to fix it. I couldn't imagine driving it with the lack of power steering, air bags and seatbelts. I certainly wouldn't let my daughters ride in the car.

After calling my dad to see if he wanted the Mustang, he told me I should sell it. I did. David came to Central Florida and bought the car from me. He flipped it a few weeks later for considerably more than he paid. Of course, every visit after that my dad lamented the Mustang's sale.

"We should have kept that old car and fixed it up." He'd tell me.

"Dad, you aren't strong enough to even turn the steering wheel anymore." I'd remind him that he didn't select the power steering option.

My dad had the same sentimental feelings about the Chevrolet S-10 pickup (which had thumbtacks holding up the headliner) and the ragged pontoon boat that he sold. So, Dad saying he missed the Mustang didn't bother me too much. He was just attached to the memories.

A lot changes in fifty years. A boy grows up and has children and grandchildren of his own. A town evolves and businesses come and go. The population and traffic continue to grow. Some of the conversations, however, remain the same:

"Scotty, have you ever seen a day as hot as this one?"

"Nope... I ain't never seen a day as hot as this."

I expected to retire and live in Sopchoppy like my dad, Uncle Dan and Aunt Jo Ann did. During the first decade of my employment in Titusville, I sketched out house plans for the Indian Summer lot next to my dad's. I guess I never thought about my dad not living there when I retired.

As I grew older, my retirement goal changed as well.

In 2022 the Strickland Family lost Aunt Jo Ann, Uncle Dan and my dad. All in the same year. They were all in their eighties when they died of natural causes. Aunt Jo Ann died in January, Uncle Dan in June and my dad right after his birthday in September.

My dad's health was deteriorating, but I never expected his death to come so soon after I visited him a few weeks before his birthday. He played the pig-dice game, Pass the Pig, with Lisa and I at the dining room table. Even smiled when he "cheated" by rolling over a pig to get more points.

I was told that he wouldn't get out of bed on his birthday. By the time I got to Sopchoppy, he was completely bedridden at home and almost non-verbal. Friends and family came to visit him during his last days. Hymns were sung. All his children were around him when Dad died.

Aunt Jo Ann, Uncle Dan and Dad are all in Heaven now, with Mema and Grandaddy, waiting on their families.

In this book I tell a lot of stories about my dad. In some, as a teenager, I pushed my dad to be angry or yell at me. Conflict makes good stories. Rest assured that those times were the exception. My dad never did anything more than yell or give me an occasional swift college ring "thump". My punishments were usually extra chores or losing my driving privileges. For every time he yelled at me calling me "boy", there are a hundred times where he hugged me and told me, "I love you son."

In the final decades of my dad's life, he looked forward to being around his grandchildren. He was a sweeter, more tolerant man. He made it to church more often than not. When he knew he was in his last years, he wanted to pass down things that were important to him. He smiled when he gave me his FSU college ring.

Later, he made a special trip to my home in Central Florida to give me his Browning A5 12-gauge shotgun. My mom gave him that gun for Christmas the year before their divorce. It was the same shotgun he brought during our deer "hunting trips" with Bobby Jack and Bully. The shotgun is in excellent condition, having rarely been fired.

My visits to Sopchoppy are shorter and less frequent than I would like. Even in retirement, it seems we are busier than ever. I visit Leona and my brother and sisters as often as I can.

With so much family and friends still in Sopchoppy, somebody invariably calls me out when I'm in town or at church.

"Hey Scotty!" they'll greet me.

I then struggle to remember their names. I can usually remember their surname or their parents. Their last names are either Strickland, Langston, Lawhon or Vause... I know.

"I knew it was you! you look just like your daddy!" is the next thing they say.

Stacey, Mom, Dad and Scott at the Trailer

About the Author

George "Scott" Strickland is a native Floridian that grew up in Tallahassee and Sopchoppy, Florida. He also lived in Berea, Kentucky, where he went to high school.

Scott graduated from Florida State University with a degree in Mechanical Engineering. He also has a master's degree in engineering management from Florida Tech. He was an engineer and manager working at Kennedy Space Center for 35 years. His teams developed complex ground support equipment for the International Space Station, Space Launch System and many other space programs. Among many NASA recognitions for his efforts, he was awarded a Silver Snoopy in 2011.

Scott is enthusiastic about FIRST robotics and has been a mentor of high school students since 1997. He was the recipient of the Regional Woodie Flowers award in 2006.

Scott lives with his wife Lisa in Central Florida, and they travel around the country in their camper van to visit National Parks and their grandchildren.

www.ingramcontent.com/pod-product-compliance
Ingram Content Group UK Ltd.
Pitfield, Milton Keynes, MK11 3LW, UK
UKHW041953190726
13854UKWH00005B/1936